SHOW
ME THE
MONEY!

SHOW
ME THE
MONEY!

How to make money from
sports marketing

ESTEVE CALZADA

B L O O M S B U R Y
LONDON • NEW DELHI • NEW YORK • SYDNEY

Note

While every effort has been made to ensure that the content of this book is as technically accurate and as sound as possible, neither the author nor the publishers can accept responsibility for any injury or loss sustained as a result of the use of this material.

Published by Bloomsbury Publishing Plc
50 Bedford Square
London WC1B 3DP

www.bloomsbury.com

First published in Spain in 2012 by Libros de Cabecera S.L. under the same title

This translated edition published 2013

ISBN (print): 978-1-4729-0302-0

ISBN (ePdf): 978-1-4729-0303-7

ISBN (EPUB): 978-1-4729-0304-4

A CIP catalogue record for this book is available from the British Library.

Acknowledgements
Cover art, inside photographs and illustrations from the Spanish edition
Translated by Anna Balaguer
Commissioned by Charlotte Croft

This book is produced using paper that is made from wood grown in managed, sustainable forests. It is natural, renewable and recyclable. The logging and manufacturing processes conform to the environmental regulations of the country of origin.

Typeset in URW Grotesk and Rockwell by seagulls.net

For Maria Rosa, for always being with me.

For Carol, for being so responsible and persevering.

For Esteve, for infecting me with his joy each day.

For my parents, for everything they have done for me.

Contents

Introduction

In January 2002, one of my dreams came true when I was appointed chief commercial and marketing officer for FC Barcelona. Back then, although I already had 12 years' experience working in international and fast moving consumer goods marketing, my knowledge of the football business was practically nil.

I took on a huge responsibility at a time when the club was under extreme pressure, in terms of both match results and finances, and initially I did so by applying common sense and management methods from other industries in which I'd worked and also by observing the work of other pioneering clubs of the time (particularly Manchester United and Real Madrid). I searched for books about methodology and for case studies taken from European football. All I found were books written from the perspective of the major American professional leagues, which were hardly going to be of much use to me in my new office at the Camp Nou.

So, condemned to practice a completely self-taught management style, I embarked on my professional career in the dynamic world of sports management.

Why did I write this book?

More than eleven years have passed since I started at Barça, and in my current position as CEO of Prime Time Sport (the company I set up after leaving the club in mid-2007), I continue to receive queries about whether there are any good books out there about sports marketing as it applies to Europe and to football. The answer to these queries (there are no such books), the suggestions I have had from followers on social networking sites and my keenness to share over a decade of experience have driven me to take the decision to write this book.

The purpose of *Show Me the Money!* is also to help to create a positive and optimistic climate for the future of the unique industry that is football, in the midst of a generally fatalistic discourse on its economic situation and sustainability. So we shall be talking about revenue and growth instead of the costs, losses and debts that are suffocating many sports organisations. After many years of overspending, bad management and keeping the accounts afloat through extraordinary transactions, now is the time to grow the revenue of sport properties from their principal assets, aggressively and sustainably.

Who am I talking to?

The book (which, if it wasn't obvious by now, is 100 per cent centred on the world of football) analyses the possibilities created by sports marketing when it comes to generating revenue for a football sport property (such as a tournament, a federation, a club or an individual athlete) and it does so by using a direct, informative style. In this way, it aims to be of interest to various groups, such as:

▶ Students and professionals of other industries who want to work in sports marketing.
▶ Sports journalists.
▶ Executives in companies that have business links with sport properties.
▶ People who already work in sports management and want to broaden or update their knowledge.

How is this book organised?

Show Me the Money! has 14 chapters grouped into four parts. Part I unpicks the big numbers involved in the sports industry, general definitions and concepts that will be used throughout the book, and describes the important process of defining the strategy and positioning of a sports property. It is in this part that we present the sports marketer's roadmap, which will serve as a compass for the book and a framework for organising all the big concepts it includes.

Part II includes the activities aimed at generating positive media exposure and capturing a critical mass of fans: key aspects that are the first step in developing revenue-generation projects, which are included in Part III, where we take a look at the main pillars of sports marketing revenue, such as use of the stadium (including a case study of Italian club Juventus), sponsorship, players' image rights, television rights and the management of licensed products (merchandise).

Part IV focuses on aspects relating to how contracts are agreed and implemented, with an emphasis on the capital importance of developing a customer service mentality that is often notable for its absence in sports properties. This final part also has a chapter devoted to sponsorship, which includes case studies of Audi, Nike, Coca-Cola and Mahou.

Finally, the very last chapter looks at the team and the sales techniques and skills needed to aspire to success in the world of sports marketing, as well as the information one must gather when starting a new project as a manager of a sports organisation.

Show Me the Money! does not set out to preach a doctrine on how things *have* to be done, nor to be a biography about my professional experience at FC Barcelona (although for those interested in a behind-the-scenes look at the club there is lots to learn). It does aim to provide the sports marketer (the name we give to the commercial and marketing manager of a sports property) with a simple method for organising ideas and actions relating to revenue generation. In the *Show me the tactics* section at the end of each chapter and in the *Coach's notebook* boxes, I provide to-do lists for each activity and a set of practical tips based both on my own experiences and on other real-life examples.

I shall end this introduction by referring to the reasons that led me to choose the title of this book. The people who have worked with me throughout my career know that I wholeheartedly identify with the *Show Me the Money!* philosophy inspired by the famous quote from the film *Jerry Maguire*. Because the ultimate purpose is, of course, to seek out and obtain continuous revenue for our sports property. So, let's get down to work, sports marketer. The money is waiting. Show me the money, there's no time to lose.

PART I

ANALYSIS, STRATEGY AND POSITIONING

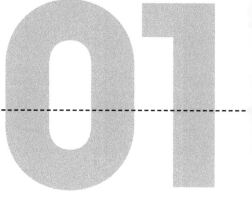

Sport and business

'Sport is too much of a game to be a business and too much of a business to be a game.'

This statement, taken from the book *Principles and Practice of Sport Management* (Masteralexis, Barr and Hums), sums up the peculiar business of sport perfectly. The interest that sport generates in fans all over the world has made it into a huge business. And because it is a game and a form of entertainment, it creates extra emotional pressure for the people who are meant to take the decisions in this business.

As can be seen in the chart below, sport is followed by the majority of adults in the world's major economies.

PERCENTAGE OF THE ADULT POPULATION THAT REGULARLY FOLLOWS SPORT

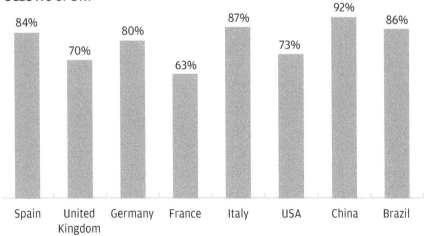

Source: Global Sports Media Consumption Report 2011 (Perform, TV Sports Markets & KantarSport)

We shall be devoting this first chapter to looking at the big numbers involved in the world of sport and to familiarising ourselves with the major sports institutions and the different models of ownership. Then, as we start to focus on football, we will be taking a look at the current economic context and will learn about the big strategy decisions taken by managers.

Football, king of sports

There is no doubt that, as can be seen in the table below, football is Europe's most popular sport.

SPORTS WITH THE BIGGEST FOLLOWING IN EACH COUNTRY

	1	2	3	4	5
Spain	Football (67%)	Formula 1 (51%)	Tennis (47%)	Basketball (37%)	Moto GP (35%)
United Kingdom	Football (41%)	Formula 1 (30%)	Cricket (23%)	Tennis (21%)	Rugby (19%)
Germany	Football (54%)	Formula 1 (37%)	Boxing (30%)	Skiing (23%)	Athletics (22%)
France	Football (31%)	Rugby (25%)	Tennis (23%)	Formula 1 (17%)	Cycling (16%)
Italy	Football (61%)	Formula 1 (44%)	Moto GP (40%)	Swimming (30%)	Cycling (27%)
USA	NFL (42%)	Baseball (35%)	Basketball (31%)	Football (19%)	NASCAR (17%)
China	Table tennis (50%)	Basketball (49%)	Badminton (47%)	Football (44%)	Swimming (43%)
Brazil	Football (68%)	Formula 1 (48%)	Volleyball (45%)	Swimming (32%)	Gymnastics (28%)

Source: Global Sports Media Consumption Report 2011 (Perform, TV Sports markets & KantarSport)

If we take a closer look at the table, we can draw some conclusions about the factors that may help to explain the differences between fans' interests in different countries. Let's see:

❶ The presence of 'national heroes' has a strong impact on the promotion of a particular sport. Legendary racing drivers such as Fernando Alonso, Michael Schumacher and Ayrton Senna have markedly increased the popularity of Formula 1 across the world and in their home countries. Ferrari, too, has a lot to do with the success of this sport in Italy. In other sports, Yao Ming is, without a doubt, the main driver behind the growth of basketball in China.

❷ History and tradition also play a fundamental role in fans' preferences. The popularity of cricket in the United Kingdom, rugby in France and the NFL in the United States have hindered the penetration of other sports, as it is so difficult to change the habits of sports consumers.

❸ The countries that host major events have a greater number of followers of that sport. This is the case with, for example, tennis in France, thanks to the Roland Garros tournament (the French Open).

❹ Finally, it is interesting to see that despite the efforts of the big European teams (and their recurring physical presence, in the form of promotional tours), football is having a hard time climbing the ranks in two of the world's largest markets: the United States and China.

And when we review the figures obtained when comparing revenue from the Olympic Games and the FIFA World Cup, for example, or the TV audiences of different sporting events, we once again see the global dominance and sheer scale of football.

REVENUE OF THE OLYMPIC GAMES BEIJING 2008 VS FIFA WORLD CUP SOUTH AFRICA 2010

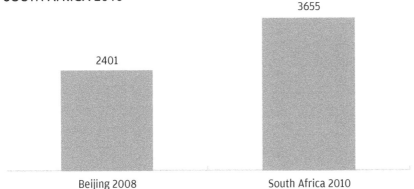

Source: IOC and FIFA
Figures in millions of US dollars

GLOBAL TV VIEWING FIGURES

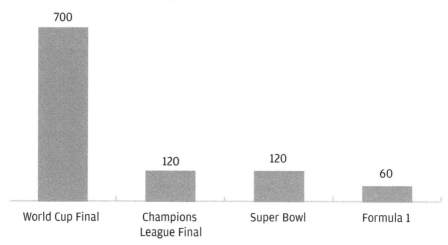

Source: Prime Time Sport
Figures in millions of viewers

Sports properties

After that quick look at the numbers, let's focus in on football's sport 'properties'. By this we mean the entities or athletes that, because of their size, history, social impact, silverware or personality, have the potential needed to build their own product portfolio. We will be looking at all the products that generate revenue in light of this concept of 'sports property', because this is the principal beneficiary of sports marketing work.

Sports properties fall into four main groups:

❶ **Tournaments or championships**, be they official or friendly in nature, that are held recurrently with the participation of several teams, regardless of size, organiser or competition format. In this category, we can include elite tournaments such as the FIFA World Cup, the UEFA European Championship and Champions League, major league championships and cups and friendly tournaments (such as the Emirates Cup or the Amsterdam Tournament). It also includes lower-division championships (i.e. lower category or lower age) and more local tournaments.

MOST IMPORTANT FOOTBALL TOURNAMENTS IN THE WORLD

Competition	Participants	Owner	Revenue*
World Cup	National teams	FIFA	2592 (2010)
European Championship	National teams	UEFA	1300 (2008)
Champions League	Clubs	UEFA	1140 (2010/11)
Copa América	National teams	CONMEBOL	N/A
Copa Libertadores	Clubs	CONMEBOL	N/A
Premier League	Clubs	Clubs	2917 (2011/12)
Bundesliga	Clubs	Clubs	1872 (2011/12)
La Liga BBVA	Clubs	Clubs	1765 (2011/12)
Serie A	Clubs	Clubs	1570 (2011/12)
Ligue 1	Clubs	Clubs	1136 (2011/12)

Source: FIFA, UEFA, Deloitte
* Revenue in millions of euros (exchange rate €1 = $1.41)

❷ **National teams** – football teams made up of players of the same nationality, organised into different age groups. National football federations also fall into this group, because they are responsible for their national team.

FIFA RANKING OF NATIONAL TEAMS

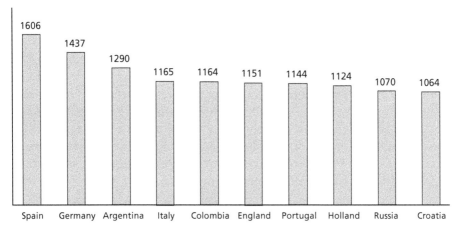

Source: FIFA, January 2013
Figures in points

❸ **Clubs** – teams or groups of teams, generally privately owned, whose daily activities generate the opportunity to market different products and services. According to the report published annually by Deloitte, the ten most important clubs in Europe when it comes to revenue are:

TOP 10 EUROPEAN CLUBS IN TERMS OF REVENUE

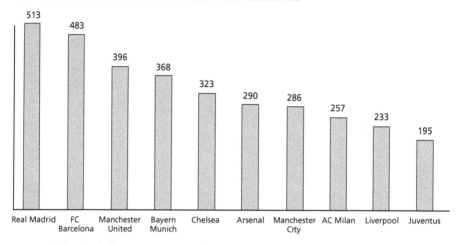

Source: Deloitte Football Money League 2011/12
Figures in millions of euros
Not including sales of players

❹ **Footballers.** Independently of their role in the other categories, on an individual level football players can also be considered sports properties with their own potential to market products (see chart opposite).

Models of ownership

I am often surprised by the actions taken by the owners of certain sports properties when they make business decisions that are – as far as I can tell – based on dubious business logic or financial profitability. I can think of numerous example of owners that are able to spend the amount it would cost to build a new stadium on a single signing; directors who reject offers for their players that could not logically be refused; major teams that help lesser teams to grow and compete against them; and companies that sponsor the kit of football teams that do not necessarily fit into their marketing strategy. This is because the football industry presents different scenarios in which return on investment is not the only goal that owners are pursuing.

Let's run through the six different models of ownership, many of them specific to the world of sport, which translate into very different strategic objectives.

FOOTBALLERS WITH THE HIGHEST MEDIA VALUE

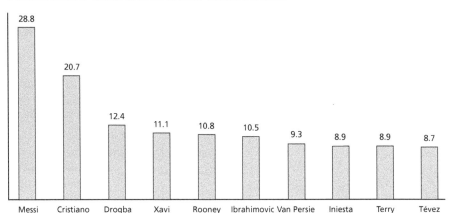

Source: University of Navarra, June 2012
Media value points as multiple of footballers' average
The ranking is of players from 100 countries

❶ **Federative model.** Most of the principal governing bodies and individuals driving the world of football. Clubs, players, referees and coaches democratically participate in the decision-making process of the federations of which they are members and these federations join up to make federative organisations that cover a larger area. Going from the lowest to the highest level of affiliation, we have the regional, national and international federations (UEFA, CONMEBOL, etc.) right up to the highest level federation: FIFA. The purpose of federations, which describe themselves as non-profit organisations, is to promote football in general and support weaker federations.

❷ **Collective model.** This model includes associations of professional clubs, such as the German Bundesliga, the English Premier League and the Spanish Liga de Fútbol Profesional (LFP). Other organisations that do not arrange competitions are included in this group, such as, for example, the European Clubs Association (ECA). The goal of these associations is based on collectively defending the interests of the member clubs.

❸ **Associative model.** Non-profit entities, in which the members are the legitimate owners, are involved in strategy decisions (using the particular system set out by each organisation), and elect the president and board of directors. In the Spanish Primera División, or La Liga, there are four football clubs that subscribe to this model: Real Madrid, FC Barcelona, Osasuna and Athletic Bilbao. There are clubs that use this model in other countries too, such as Turkey's Galatasaray. In the associative model, entities are managed on the basis of objectives such as achieving sporting success or developing initiatives and services to achieve member satisfaction.

❹ Multiple ownership. This model encompasses the football clubs in which ownership is spread across a large number of small shareholders who, as a general rule, are fans of the club. This category would include, for example, the public limited sports companies in Spanish football, such as Atlético Madrid, Valencia CF and Sevilla CF. In the multiple ownership model, the shareholders that accumulate the greatest percentage of shares (as direct owners or through the support of other shareholders) have ultimate responsibility for governing the club. In this case, the owners' principal objectives are both achieving sporting success and securing financial support for the club (often/usually based on an emotional connection to it).

❺ Single ownership. All or the vast majority of club shares are in the hands of a single person or company that has injected considerable amounts of money that will be hard to recoup through the natural workings of the club. In Europe, we have the examples of Roman Abramovich at Chelsea, Sheikh Mansour at Manchester City FC, Silvio Berlusconi at AC Milan, Massimo Moratti at Inter Milan and, more recently, the Qatari investors that have bought Malaga FC and Paris Saint-Germain. In South America, and in Mexico in particular, it is also very common for clubs to be owned by large corporations, for instance the club América, which is owned by the broadcasting giant Televisa, and Santos Laguna, owned by the Grupo Modelo (manufacturers of Corona beer). In all these cases, the owners have made big financial investments that they hope to capitalise on, obtaining added benefits such as:

▶ Public recognition and presence.
▶ Synergies with other companies they own and advertising returns for these companies.
▶ Sporting successes (mainly for the impact that this will have on the two previous points).

❻ Listing on the stock exchange. This model is a combination of models 4 and 5, with the added factor that some of the shares are listed on the stock exchange where they are freely transferred between buyers and sellers. In this group, we find clubs such as Arsenal (London), Borussia (Dortmund) and Juventus (Turin). This model is clearly in decline because of the pressure that the sporting activities put on the price of the shares.

It can lead to value swings that are unjustifiable from the point of view of the actual financial value of the club's assets. In Europe, there are currently 20 or so clubs listed on the stock exchange, a far cry from the 50 there used to be in the 1980s and 1990s.

The different models of ownership in football create an interesting array of strategic objectives. In models 4, 5 and 6 the usual business objectives are present, such as dividend returns or the sale of shares at a higher price than they were bought for. So, although we may find other objectives, in all the ownership models, the property will be continuously exercising pressure to increase revenue, and this is precisely the objective that we are concerned with.

Football finance

It's no news to anyone that the football industry currently finds itself in a somewhat delicate financial situation. In this section we will look at the four factors that have led to these economic difficulties and how they condition the way sports properties are managed.

❶ **Accelerated growth.** Increasing demand for the most popular sport on the planet has led to a spectacular and widespread growth in revenue. Globalisation, the ever-rising value of TV rights and the sale of players at exorbitant prices at one point filled the coffers of sports properties, attracting new owners from other industries and geographical areas.

GROWTH OF REVENUE IN THE MAJOR EUROPEAN LEAGUES

Competition	Revenue 1999/2000	Revenue 2011/12	Total growth (annual growth)
English Premier League	1219	2917	+139% (7.5%)
German Bundesliga	681	1872	+175% (8.8%)
Spanish Primera División	722	1765	+144% (7.7%)
Italian Serie A	954	1570	+65% (4.2%)
French Ligue 1	607	1136	+87% (5.4%)
Total	4183	9260	+121% (6.8%)

Source: Deloitte Annual Review of Football Finance 2013
Figures in millions of euros

❷ **Overspending.** The obsessive need to win, the emotional decisions taken by directors, the lack of professionalism and experience, and the complacency that results from revenue flowing in have translated into major sports investments (principally in the form of player signings and high salaries) that, once they surpass the income level, have led to a proliferation of accounts that are squarely in the red. Losses suffered by first division clubs in the European leagues reached the record figure of €1675 million in the 2010/11 season, 36 per cent more than in the previous year.

GROWTH IN PLAYERS' SALARIES IN THE MAJOR EUROPEAN LEAGUES (IN MILLIONS OF EUROS)

Competition	1999/2000 salaries (% of sales)	2011/12 salaries (% of sales)	Total growth (annual growth)
English Premier League	755 (61.9%)	2049 (70.2%)	+171% (8.7%)
German Bundesliga	382 (56.1%)	953 (50.9%)	+149% (7.9%)
Spanish Primera División	390 (54.0%)	1057 (59.9%)	+171% (8.7%)
Italian Serie A	660 (69.2%)	1179 (75.1%)	+79% (5.0%)
French Ligue 1	324 (53.4%)	841 (74.0%)	+160% (8.3%)
Total	2511 (60%)	6079 (65.6%)	+142% (7.6%)

Source: Deloitte Annual Review of Football Finance 2012
Figures in millions of euros

EVOLUTION OF FIRST DIVISION CLUB LOSSES IN EUROPE

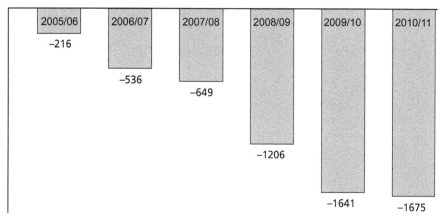

2005/06	2006/07	2007/08	2008/09	2009/10	2010/11
−216	−536	−649	−1206	−1641	−1675

Source: Club licensing benchmarking report financial year 2011, UEFA, January 2013. Figures in millions of euros

PERCENTAGE OF INVESTMENT IN SIGNINGS REPRESENTED BY THE FOUR
TEAMS THAT SPENT MOST IN EACH LEAGUE

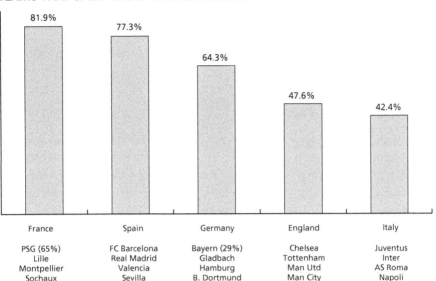

	France	Spain	Germany	England	Italy
	PSG (65%)	FC Barcelona	Bayern (29%)	Chelsea	Juventus
	Lille	Real Madrid	Gladbach	Tottenham	Inter
	Montpellier	Valencia	Hamburg	Man Utd	AS Roma
	Sochaux	Sevilla	B. Dortmund	Man City	Napoli

Source: Football Transfer Review 2013, by Prime Time Sport. 2012/13 season data.

❸ **High level of debt.** Big investments, the accumulation of losses and easy access to credit over the last few years have led to soaring levels of debt in football clubs. In Spain, for example, the joint debt of the 20 teams in La Liga surpassed €35 billion in June 2011. Against this background, a minority of clubs (Real Madrid and FC Barcelona) manage to live with their high debt levels, thanks to their ability to generate cash. However, most clubs suffer from crippling financial costs in their balance sheets as their directors work on one plan after another to refinance the debt and pay it off as late as possible.

❹ **Polarisation.** In the European transfer window of 2012/13, just ten teams made 48 per cent of the total investment in signing in the five major leagues. And in each of these leagues, just four teams monopolised more than half of the total amount invested in players.

In the case of Spain, Real Madrid and FC Barcelona made a staggering 52 per cent of the entire revenue of the top division. In England, Manchester United and Arsenal bring in 25 per cent of all Premier League revenue. These examples help to illustrate the ever-increasing gap between the big clubs and the smaller ones, between the richest and the poorest. The world of football is being polarised into two main groups: a two-speed industry. At one end of the scale we have the teams with most power, due to their public following, the financial strength of their owners or simply good management based on actual potential. On the other, we have those teams that accumulate debt because of bad management, the difficulty of accessing credit or because they have tried to compete above their station in leagues that they just cannot afford.

Management trends

In my years of experience in sports management, I have never come across such widespread consensus on the need to revise the current economic model of football. Given all this, the people responsible for regulating the management of sports properties are, as we speak, working on a new framework of action, in which three ways forward are clear:

❶ **Collective actions.** The regulatory bodies and organisers of competitions have already developed three types of measures: (i) preventive measures; (ii) mechanisms of chastisement; and (iii) actions to redistribute value. So, for example, we have the new Financial Fair Play mechanism promoted by UEFA, which will not allow loss-making or financially unhealthy clubs to take part in European competitions; or the Premier League, which penalised Portsmouth by docking nine points after they had gone into administration in 2010. But organisations such as FIFA or UEFA also give financial support to weaker federations, and most of the major leagues distribute their TV revenue to benefit weaker teams and set up aid funds to soften the blow that teams suffer when they are relegated.

❷ **Sports management.** Because of their influence on the results on the pitch and on the club economy, actual sport decisions are of vital importance and are geared towards competing efficiently while spending as little as possible. For example, we can see how sport directors have begun to reduce the number of players they employ, encourage greater use of home-grown players, sell off their big players or try to sign other players on free transfer deals or in the form of a loan. In this context, the big five European leagues have cut their players' payroll for three consecutive seasons (2010/11, 2011/12 and 2012/13) and in Spain, 75 per cent of signings in the summer of 2012 were made at no cost or on loan.

❸ **Finances.** As well as the search for financing and investors, and the securing of ordinary revenue, work is also being done to procure exceptional revenue, or 'windfalls', using as much creativity as possible. Real estate operations, for example (Arsenal sold apartments in Highbury for £276 million from 2009 to 2011), have in turn led to complex financial transactions in the business of managing footballers' economic rights.

The world of football has before it a great opportunity (or, let's face it, a need) to change the rules of the game and capitalise on its incredibly strong role in society. Sports properties and the owners of very different profiles and objectives will always have something in common: the need to maximise revenue, aggressively and in a sustained manner. The guardian angel is no longer around and the search for the millionaire saviour is over. It's time for the sports marketer.

SHOW ME THE TACTICS

1. Familiarise yourself with the general economic situation.
2. Draw the map of sports properties in your initial geographical area of influence.
3. Find out the objectives of the owners of different sports properties and determine your own.
4. Try to understand the reasons for other sports properties' economic success and failure.

Sports marketing and products

In this chapter, I will outline the framework of actions that a sports property needs to take on its journey towards making money. Let's start with a definition of sports marketing.

> ## Sports marketing
> Generation of revenue by developing and exploiting the principal assets of a sports property: brand, stadium, facilities, championships and athletes.

This definition is the utmost expression of the *Show Me the Money!* philosophy. This is my personal definition, and there are, of course, many other versions of this, neither better nor worse, nor more or less accurate. In my version the focus is on our ultimate purpose, the *raison d'être* of sports marketing, and that is *to make money*. But it *isn't* a matter of achieving this goal any which way. This definition of sports marketing refers to revenue that must be identified as being:

▸ **Profitable:** the costs associated with generating revenue must not put profitability at risk.
▸ **Sustainable over time:** ideally, we will be seeking revenue that we can consolidate in our accounts on a recurrent basis. For example, the sale of a sponsorship package lasting several years is more sustainable than renting out an advertising hoarding in the stadium for one or two matches.
▸ **Tangible and measurable:** revenue has to be easy to measure and to translate into the sports property's profit and loss accounts.

Hail, sports marketer!

Sports marketing and the creation of revenue for sports properties would be utterly pointless without the involvement and leadership of a sports marketer. Nice to meet you! From this moment on, you, the sports marketer, are the focus of our attention and you need to be at the service of your sports property, where you will be required to put in as much effort as you can while engaging in strategic thinking, commercial proactiveness, organisation and creativity. I shall try to help you along, providing you with methods and sharing my own experiences and what I have observed and analysed of what others have put into practice. So get ready for some hard graft, with lots of internal and public pressure. And, of course, get ready for all the fun involved in this thrilling job.

Products and customers

We're now getting down to the nitty-gritty and we'll start by talking about products and customers, words that may sound very 'cold' to those who hanker back to the old days of sports management and are more used to referring to emotions and supporters. Let's be pragmatic about this and talk about *products* (defined and measurable units) that will be offered to *customers* (people or companies with which we will be establishing an 'invoicing relationship').

The table opposite includes a list of the main products in sports marketing, grouped into categories and by target user. I find it a helpful reference for drawing up action plans or simply to observe the progress of other sports properties in the market.

Let's start by looking at the grouping on the left hand side of the table. We usually refer to a sports property's revenue by 'packaging' the products into these three main families:

❶ Stadium and season ticket holders, which basically includes the products related to commercial exploitation of the stadium, such as one-off tickets and season tickets.

❷ Commercial and marketing, made up of sponsorships, advertising, image rights and official merchandising licences.

❸ Media, including television rights, the website and social networking sites.

In my early days as a sports marketer, when it came to the second revenue group, I have vivid memories of internal meetings at FC Barcelona and interviews with journalists at which we talked about how my main mission

SPORTS MARKETING PRODUCTS BY CONCEPTS AND TYPE OF CUSTOMER

	For end consumers B2C		For companies B2B	
Stadium	Tickets	Licensed products	Concessions	VIP hospitality
	Memberships/ season tickets	Catering	Advertising	Non-sporting events
Marketing		Licensed products	Sponsorships	Merchandising licences
			Advertising	Image rights
			Matches	
Media	Website	Social networks	TV rights	Sporting prizes
	TV channel	Editorial	Advertising	Contents

was defined at the time: 'developing atypical revenue'. Back then, any revenues that didn't come from the stadium or from TV but rather from commercial and marketing was considered 'extraordinary' and outside the normal workings of the club. Of course, this concept is completely obsolete today, and we now refer to the three families of products in equal terms. Indeed, it is precisely in commercial and marketing products that the sports marketer can have the biggest impact on short-term results.

Going back to the table of products, let's take a look at an important detail we find at the top: the separation of products into two main groups, B2C and B2B, depending on who our end customer is going to be. On the one hand, we have the B2C (business to consumer) group, which includes those products that we will offer directly to the end consumer without the involvement of any intermediaries. This refers mainly to the traditional business of most sports properties, based on season tickets and one-off ticket sales. On the other hand, we have the B2B (business to business) group, where we find the products sold to companies, either because they act as intermediaries between the sports property and the end consumer or because they themselves are the end users of the products.

In the B2C group you should imagine that licensed products and catering are marked with a dotted line. Of course sports properties can manage the catering outlets in the stadium directly or can manufacture their own official merchandise, but in our action plan I shall assume that these products are managed by third parties and should therefore be considered as B2B.

The sports marketer will see that most of their time will be centred on B2B clients – in other words, companies – and the success of the search for revenue will largely depend on the results achieved by these companies. In this sense, it is important to emphasise that the sports marketer should consider the challenges faced by his B2B clients as his own. Bear in mind that if a sponsor has met his objectives, he will speak well of us to other potential sponsors; if the company holding the licence to operate the restaurants in the stadium earns a good living then it will have more money to invest in improving the facilities; just as if we provide more content than stipulated in the contract to the channel that has our TV rights, it will be easier to build that client's loyalty and renew the contract for a higher fee.

Models of revenue

Let's now look at how the *revenue* from each category is distributed in football sports properties of different sizes and with different profiles. In the following chart, we can see the percentage that each revenue family brings to the total in 'tournaments and federations' (2010 World Cup, UEFA and the English FA), in the three biggest football clubs in the world (Real Madrid, FC Barcelona and Manchester United) and in other football clubs from various countries.

If we analyse the numbers and observe what has occurred in different markets over the last few years, we can find up to seven different models; seven ways of spreading revenue in sports properties (not taking into account individual footballers).

❶ **Major federations and tournaments.** Their main source of income is television rights, thanks to their global reach. They have practically no revenue from the stadium, as this is given over to the organising committees (World Cup) or to the participating clubs (UEFA Champions League).

❷ **Global clubs.** Real Madrid, FC Barcelona and Manchester United have a revenue distribution in which the different categories are of similar size. Thus, as a result of their international expansion strategy, the weight of

DISTRIBUTION OF REVENUE IN SPORTS PROPERTIES

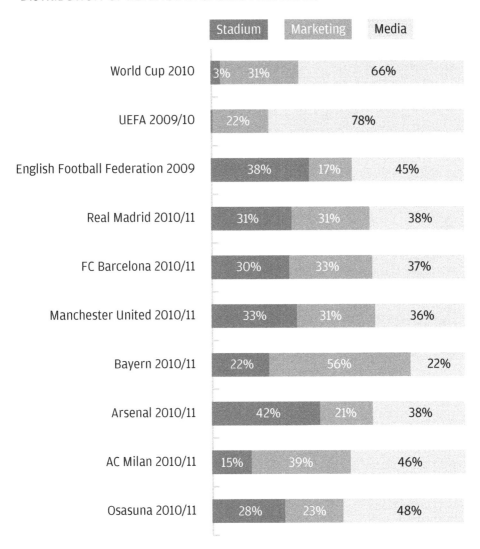

	Stadium	Marketing	Media
World Cup 2010	3%	31%	66%
UEFA 2009/10		22%	78%
English Football Federation 2009	38%	17%	45%
Real Madrid 2010/11	31%	31%	38%
FC Barcelona 2010/11	30%	33%	37%
Manchester United 2010/11	33%	31%	36%
Bayern 2010/11	22%	56%	22%
Arsenal 2010/11	42%	21%	38%
AC Milan 2010/11	15%	39%	46%
Osasuna 2010/11	28%	23%	48%

Source: FIFA; Deloitte; clubs
Does not include players or real estate (exchange rate: €1 = $1.46 = £0.87)

revenue from the stadium has gradually fallen, giving way to the ever greater weight of media and marketing revenue.

❸ **The German model.** Championed by Bayern Munich, this model has commercial revenue as its largest segment, mostly due to the strength of the domestic sponsorship market.

❹ **The English model.** Its strongest feature is the amount of revenue that comes from stadium exploitation, because of factors such as ticket sales planning and the commercial success of hospitality packages.

❺ **The Italian model.** Despite the growing trend for clubs to collectively sell their TV rights, they still solidly top the revenue of Italian clubs. The big challenge is to attract more people to the stadia.

❻ **The national model.** With TV rights the main source of income here too, this model includes professional clubs in countries with economically powerful television organisations that do not have the potential to expand internationally.

❼ **The traditional model.** This includes clubs that operate on a local level and whose television rights have no financial value. It is therefore based on ticket sales and attracting season ticket holders and sponsors in the geographical area in which the club operates on a daily basis.

MODELS OF REVENUE DISTRIBUTION IN SPORTS PROPERTIES

Models	Stadium and membership	Media	Commercial marketing
Federation/tournament	0–5%	**70–75%**	23–30%
Global club	30%	35–40%	30%
German model	20%	25%	**55%**
English model	**40–45%**	35–40%	20–25%
Italian model	10–15%	**60–65%**	25–30%
National model	30–35%	**50–55%**	20–25%
Traditional model	**80%**	0%	20%

Sports marketing vs conventional marketing

In the final part of this chapter, I shall be giving a brief and very general overview of the factors that are intrinsic to sports marketing. Although I've always thought that conventional marketing and sports marketing have more similarities than differences (this may be because I brought lots of my marketing knowledge to the sports marketing world I found myself in), the sports marketer still has to take into account a number of factors that will influence his or her daily work. These factors will bring both frustration and joy, through no fault or merit of his or her own, in the sports marketer's journey to success and money. It is all about being aware of the need to live alongside these factors, while doing your job the best you can.

I see there being ten factors or circumstances out of your control that will impact on the work of the sports marketer:

1. Sports results and the role of chance.
2. The influential role of emotions in the decision-making process.
3. The diversity of objectives set by the owners of sports properties.
4. The pressure of public opinion.
5. The difficulty of maintaining project confidentiality.
6. Group decisions or decisions made by third parties.
7. The lesser relevance of price as a key factor for boosting sales.
8. The fact that demand is subject to massive fluctuations that are often difficult to measure in advance.
9. The need to constantly battle against unfair competition coming at us from all sides.
10. The positive fact that the effort one invests in gaining a single fan is compensated by the certainty that we have that fan for life.

SHOW ME THE TACTICS

1. Identify the products already being sold by your sports property.
2. Find similar or competing sports properties and analyse their products and revenue models.
3. Use your initiative (initially) to forecast the growth potential of each revenue family and put your sports property into the right group of revenue distribution models.
4. Identify a small group of trusted stakeholders made up of sponsors, journalists, opinion leaders, merchandising licence holders and buyers of TV rights who have a vested interest in the success of the club. With them, you will be able to generate new ideas, and informally and confidentially validate your most important decisions.

03

Strategy, positioning and brand

Phone calls, messages on your BlackBerry or iPhone, emails flagged as high priority, unscheduled meetings ... a sports marketer's day at the office is replete with interruptions and it never turns out the way one thinks. That's why, in sports management, there is a tendency to concentrate one's efforts on completing tasks that are considered urgent or that have immediate results, without dedicating enough time to strategy and planning. In this chapter, we shall be looking at the intensive *strategic* work that should precede any commercial work on a sports property. Although it won't be easy to find any quality time in the midst of all the hustle and bustle, good strategic practice will bring returns on the more commercial side of the sports marketer's work.

The sports marketer's roadmap

If we have a sports property that has public relevance in a particular geographical area, or at least an idea or plan to create it, we're ready to go. Always start by checking the compass that you will be using on your exciting journey in search of money. The sports marketer's roadmap (this is the name we shall give to our own unique GPS) starts, ends and restarts with a sports property and a project. Let me explain.

The roadmap arranges the sports marketer's activities into four main phases:

❶ **Analysis, strategy and positioning.** In this phase, conduct market research, select the positioning, develop business plans and create the brand design.

❷ **Media exposure and critical mass.** This is split into two elements – the first is ensuring the continued presence in the media and in social networks of the content your sports property has generated, and the second is the need to continue to attract supporters. Fans, registered users or followers on social networks define the potential to generate revenue, which is the goal of the next phase.

❸ **Commercialisation.** Having transformed the essence of the sports property into a brand through positioning, the time will come to develop and market the family of commercial products. The roadmap concentrates on products related to stadium sales (such as one-off and season tickets), sponsorship deals, image rights of individual footballers, television rights and officially licensed merchandise. It is in this phase that the sports marketer has to put into practice their skills as a salesperson and demonstrate their ability to get money, more money and yet more money.

❹ **Implementation.** The fourth and final phase is as important as the three preceding phases, or even more so, because good implementation and after-sales service will translate into customer loyalty and greater potential to renew contracts. If I'm honest this phase includes a fair amount of the sports marketer's less fulfilling work, because with the revenue confirmed and under pressure to make even more money, you have to find the time and the resources to implement the agreements to an excellent standard, signing contracts that are an exact reflection of the agreements reached, scrupulously meeting the commitments one has taken on and developing a relationship of absolute trust with the customers, with the ultimate purpose of translating all that into contract renewals and, if possible, under more favourable terms.

One way of looking at the roadmap is that phases 1 and 2 are the marketing work of the sports marketer (office-based work), while phases 3 and 4 include the more commercial-type activities (fieldwork).

Through my experience over the years, I can confidently say that the major areas for improvement in the way sports properties are currently managed are undoubtedly the insufficient time allocated to the tasks included in the first and last phases. In practice, most time is concentrated on the relationship with the media, on pulling in supporters and on sales, where the results are much more tangible in the short term. But with good initial strategy work and the subsequent implementation, the chances of getting higher and more long-term revenue will, without a shadow of a doubt, be much greater.

Here's the roadmap in graphic form. Remember that the process I've described is a recurrent one: a compass or mental organiser that never goes away; a process that never ends. Bear in mind that, although you may wish to follow the sequence of activities included in the roadmap to the letter, in practice you will always find yourself carrying out tasks from all four phases

PHASES IN THE SPORTS MARKETER'S ROADMAP

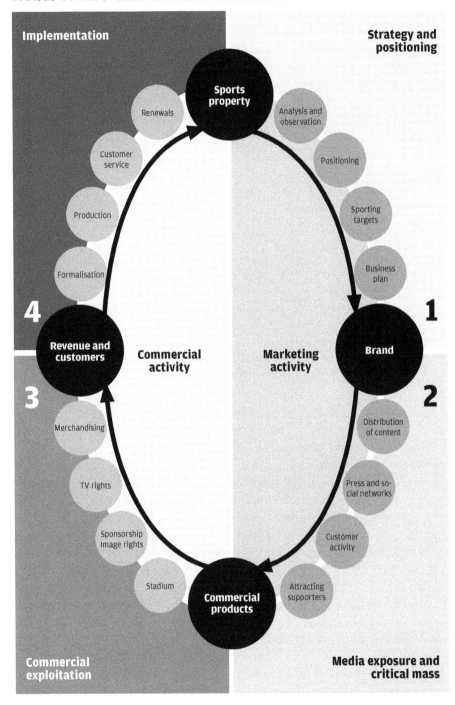

simultaneously. This is to be expected, given that the pressure to generate revenue is there from day one to the very end and that management won't give a monkey's about roadmaps or phases. The only thing you need to do, even if it's just mentally, is to place what you are doing at any given time into its corresponding phase and not give in to the temptation to not devote enough time to the first and final phases.

Let's now look in detail at all the tasks involved in developing the strategy and the positioning, which will make up the first phase of the indispensable roadmap.

We need positioning

I have mentioned this word several times now and have not yet stopped to explain what it means. Here's a theoretical definition:

Positioning

A set of statements or ideas used to describe the targeted image perceived by supporters (B2C) and clients (B2B) of a sports property in relation to its competitors.

The process of positioning is one of the most important and difficult decisions a sports marketer has to make. The extremely dynamic and competitive environment creates the need for strategies that do not change over time and that make us different from our competitors, so that we can keep these strategies in mind every time we need to make a decision. These strategy points are what we find in the positioning of a sports property.

I will never forget the first match I went to at Anfield, the legendary Liverpool FC stadium. It was 6 March 2007 and, despite winning 1-0 (with a goal from Guðjohnsen), FC Barcelona was eliminated from the Champions League (with Liverpool winning on away goals after winning the previous match 2-1). The Liverpool fans sang the anthemic 'You'll Never Walk Alone' at the end of the match, and then something quite unexpected happened. While the Barça fans were waiting for the police to let them leave the stadium, the Liverpool fans began chanting 'Barça! Barça! Barça!' At that moment, the sadness of elimination gave way to the emotion of that unique situation. The Liverpool fans were paying tribute to the Barça fans.

Liverpool FC, therefore, has a line of positioning in the way it uses its unique fan base, and there are lots of other examples of clear positioning – the Brazilian national football team stands out for its magical players and playing style, and the upbeat joyousness with which the country is associated; Athletic Bilbao competes in La Liga with exclusively Basque players; the Premier League is known for the intensive involvement of its fans in matches and for the rigidity of its regulations; FC Barcelona decided to become the most charitable institution in the world of football; Mario Balotelli is thought of as a 'bad boy of football'; Ajax of Amsterdam selects young players and opts for an offensive game; and the UEFA Champions League is the 'perfect' competition. These are just a few examples of positioning lines used by different sports properties; some of them are the result of historical circumstances while others are the consequence of decisions made by their executives.

To choose the positioning of a sports property, you need to follow these phases of actions: (1) analysis of the history and traditions; (2) identification of positioning lines; (3) drawing up the positioning map; (4) selection; (5) implementation.

Let's go through each of them in detail.

❶ **Analysis of the history and traditions.** As well as being a lot of fun, delving into the past is an essential first step in the process of selecting the positioning. The sports marketer should meticulously analyse any available information on the origins and evolution of the sports property. For example, with a club, study how it was founded, the key characters, noteworthy moments and situations, aspects relating to the home city, iconic players, fans' activities, classic matches, style of play, sports statistics, opinion polls and any other factor that, through media coverage, may have influenced public opinion and perception. The result of this analysis will be a source of inspiration when drawing up the options, and it will also help to identify the crown jewels that must be respected and not tampered with.

Let's look at a few examples of key historical events at different sports properties. They may provide inspiration when developing your own market positioning:

▶ Andrés Iniesta made millions of Spaniards happy when he scored the winning goal against Holland in extra time at the final of the World Cup in South Africa 2010, giving Spain its first ever World Cup.
▶ The founders of Sport Lisboa e Benfica of Portugal decided to include an eagle on the club badge to symbolise its authority, independence and nobility.
▶ In 1963, Liverpool FC fans began singing the song 'You'll Never Walk Alone' at the beginning of every match played at Anfield.
▶ The final of the UEFA Champions League 2005, held at the Atatürk Olympic Stadium in Istanbul, was the most thrilling in history, as

Liverpool FC came back from nowhere to equal AC Milan's three goals and ended up winning the penalty shoot-out.

▶ Boca Juniors of Buenos Aires (Argentina) would not be what it is without its legendary La Bombonera stadium.

▶ Footballers such as Di Stéfano, Zidane, Ronaldo and Cristiano Ronaldo, among others, got into the Spanish League because Real Madrid builds up its teams by trying to sign the best players in the world.

▶ Paris Saint-Germain is the most important club in the French capital, a city that is renowned globally as one of the most attractive cities in the world.

▶ The Dutch national side earned itself the nickname 'the Clockwork Orange' after steamrolling Argentina 4-0 in a second-stage match in the World Cup in Germany 1974, during which the Argentine team only took the ball over the halfway line once.

▶ In 2011, FC Barcelona played in the finals of the Club World Cup in Japan and the UEFA Champions League with nine and seven home-grown players, respectively, out of the starting 11.

❷ **Identifying the positioning lines.** The next step will lead us to deciding on the lines that we shall use to position our sports property in relation to the competition. Although there are no positioning lines that are common to all types of sports properties, we can highlight the seven variables that are used most frequently:

Ⓐ **The geographical line.** This is the line that links the sports property to its country/city of origin, with the traditions and character of the people that go with it. This would be the case for the Brazilian national side (the country being an attractive tourist destination with people seen as 'joyful') or Paris Saint-Germain, with all the charm of Paris (and where the Eiffel Tower is even depicted on the club badge), or Sevilla FC, whose directors often say that they are 'Sevilla fans in Andalusia, Andalusian in Spain and Spaniards in Europe'. This is one of the most cross-functional variables, as it can be used across properties – from major tournaments, national sides and clubs to individual footballers.

Ⓑ **The supporters.** This is typically used by national sides and football clubs whose fan base has a high level of involvement and a special way of supporting the team. In this case, the positioning is built by extolling season ticket holders, members and supporters, encouraging them to take part in the daily activities of the sports property and gauging their views (as much as possible) on the more important management decisions. As we have noted, Liverpool FC is one of the clubs that can use its supporters as a central piece in its positioning. Atlético Madrid does this too: this club can boast that its ticket holder numbers actually increased after it was relegated to the second division in 2000.

- **Charity.** In September 2006, FC Barcelona changed the world of football when it announced its partnership with UNICEF, and began wearing the organisation's logo on its first team's match shirts. As well as having advertising on its shirt for the first time in its history (and this crucially granted to the charity free of charge), the club committed itself to donating 0.7 per cent of its revenue to UNICEF for use in its humanitarian work. Bearing in mind that, around that time, I myself had been negotiating with several companies that were offering large sums of money to advertise their brand on the shirt, it is obvious that FC Barcelona made the landmark, high-impact decision to capitalise on the *charitable* positioning line. This support for the needy is frequently used in the world of elite football, as it serves to counteract the image of monetary excess that is often conveyed by some sports properties. So it is very common to see the most famous footballers on the planet participating in aid campaigns, or FIFA executives handing over cheques to help build schools and football pitches in developing countries. As well as FC Barcelona, clubs such as the Argentine Boca Juniors or the Italian Fiorentina have also opted for this angle. It is a relevant but not particularly differential positioning.

- **The sporting line.** The sporting aspect offers positioning opportunities that do differentiate but are also risky at the same time. For example, the sports marketer could position a national side or a football club along the line of its players' aggressiveness and fight (the 'fury' of the Spanish national side), its colourful style of play and attack (the 'total football' of Arsenal), or the make-up of its team (Athletic Bilbao only using Basque players). But bear in mind that the key to positioning is its continuity *over time*. When it comes to the pitch we run the risk of selecting a line that we cannot be sure to fulfil in the future, simply because we do not know which managers and players will be on the market at a price we can afford. Besides, the sports director and manager have a single goal: to win. Any terms and conditions that impact on how this is achieved will not be readily accepted.

- **Excellence.** It seems obvious that if something is worth doing, it's worth doing well, so using excellence as a line of positioning may seem self-evident. But in an industry where mistakes are often made because decisions are taken too quickly or simply because of a lack of qualified staff, the sports properties that are committed to conveying excellence and an eye for detail in all their activities will definitely stand out above the others. This is the case of the UEFA Champions League or the English Premier League, whose perfectionist image is an ideal advert for winning over big sponsors, for example. Use of this line by national sides or clubs has one disadvantage: it is difficult to apply it repeatedly in the sports arena, so it tends to be more suitable for 'excellent' tournaments or leagues, which do not depend on one team's results on the pitch.

❻ The legend. Those sports properties that in the past have achieved major sporting success (because of the scale of a one-off success or the recurrence of wins) can use a positioning line around the legend that is within the reach of very few competitors and that is also permanent. Real Madrid is, and always will be, thought of as a legendary team thanks to the nine European Cups/UEFA Champions League titles it has in its cabinet, five of which were won consecutively. Bayern Munich (which in the 1970s won three consecutive European Cups), the members of the Spanish side that won its first ever World Cup in 2010 (especially its manager, Vicente del Bosque; Iker Casillas, the captain who lifted the trophy; and Iniesta as the man who scored the winning goal in the final) and the Manchester United team that won the 'treble' in 1999 (Premier League, FA Cup and Champions League) are other examples of this 'legendary' angle.

❼ Personality. When positioning footballers study their personality and behaviour on and off the pitch. Attributes that can be specifically associated with an individual player makes the sports marketer's work of finding the player's own, distinct space much easier. For example, Wayne Rooney is notable for his 'bad boy' image, while Leo Messi comes across in comparison as a very down-to-earth person.

In the table below is a summary of which positioning lines fit best into different types of sports property.

LINES OF POSITIONING AND SPORTS PROPERTIES

Positioning lines	Tournaments	National sides	Clubs	Footballers
Geographical	•	•	•	•
Supporters		•	•	
Charity	•	•	•	•
Sport		•	•	•
Excellence	•			
Legend		•	•	
Personality				•

❸ **Drawing up the positioning map.** In the next phase, we shall be putting the work we have done up to now into context, and include our competitors in this process. We shall be drawing a map (even if only a mental one) on which we shall place our competitors along the positioning lines that we have considered most relevant to our sports property. The aim is to find unoccupied or relatively untravelled 'spaces' on this map that can help us to differentiate ourselves from our main rivals.

Let's put this into practice with a real case study, that of Manchester City FC. The major investment in players made by the Arab owners took the club into the Champions League and placed it in the 'elite' of clubs fighting for the big titles (indeed, Manchester City won the FA Cup in 2011 and were the Premier League champions in 2012). With this outlook of further future sporting success, Manchester City would be able to draw up an international expansion plan, for which it would need to develop a positioning that would let it attract supporters and B2B clients in new markets. Obviously, this plan has to find the way to differentiate the club from its other big rivals that have precisely the same goal. So for this case specifically, we could draw a map using the following lines of positioning: (1) geographical; (2) charitable; (3) legendary; (4) sporting; and (5) supporters. Having placed some of the main competitors, the positioning map might look something like this:

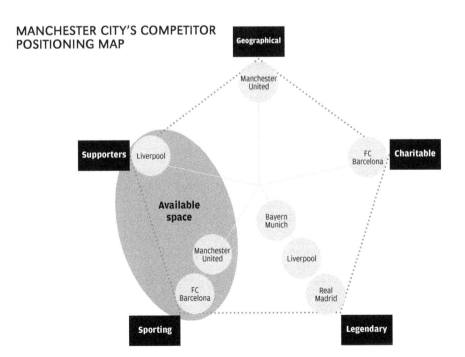

MANCHESTER CITY'S COMPETITOR POSITIONING MAP

From studying this map you can see that the 'geographical' and 'charitable' lines do not offer any ownership opportunities in the short term. On the one hand, Manchester United occupies the geographical space as the club of the city of Manchester (even though Manchester City FC is in the city too) and on the other, FC Barcelona (which first hit upon the high-impact UNICEF project) occupies the charity space. If we follow the map around clockwise, we find the 'legend' line, crowded by the big trophy-winning clubs, and which one can only access in the very long term (we're talking of periods of at least ten years). On the 'sporting' line of the map, we have put FC Barcelona because of its style of play and selection of home-grown players. Bearing in mind that Manchester City is one of the Premier League teams with the most English players in the squad and that it is planning to build a spectacular academy in which to generate new talent, we could find some available space along this line. Finally, we have the 'supporters' line, which is occupied by Liverpool FC on this map (for reasons we have already explained). It is also an interesting space that Manchester City could consider, because its supporters do have some features that make them unique. For example, at the matches I've attended at the Etihad Stadium in Manchester, I've noted the fans passionately singing 'Blue Moon' (Manchester City's home kit is sky blue) at the beginning and end of the match, and as a way of celebrating their goals.

The selected positioning should be ...

❶ **Unique.** You will by now recognise the need to choose a position that differentiates the property from the competition.

❷ **Feasible.** It has to be a realistic position – compatible with the sports property's possibilities and taking into account historical factors.

❸ **Long-lasting.** The longer this position can be adhered to, or with minimal tweaks, the greater the contribution it will make to the marketing strategy.

❹ **Relevant.** It has to be founded on content that is of interest both to the general public and to clients in particular.

❺ **Easy to explain and understand.** Can the positioning be described by using simple language, in a few phrases and with few words in each phrase? If not, then it's too complicated.

❻ **Open to nuance.** The mission statement needs to be written with enough scope to give some room for manoeuvre in its application and everyday use.

❹ Selection. This initial analytical work must guide us into making a decision on which direction (or directions) to follow. At this point, positioning moves from the abstract to the tangible, by using a set of statements that over time will become the guiding principle in all the sports property's management decisions.

Positioning of FC Barcelona

I was fortunate enough to be, from start to finish, a member of the team that developed a new positioning statement for FC Barcelona, which involved the process we have covered in this section, as part of a new international expansion plan for the club. We were starting out late in comparison with other major clubs such as Real Madrid and Manchester United, and we needed to design a proposal for supporters that was different to the rest. So we defined two very specific lines of positioning: (1) charity and (2) spectacular football. The actual, formal phrasing looked something like this:

❶ FC Barcelona is the club most deeply committed to social causes:
- ▶ It drives social actions, with a particular focus on children.
- ▶ It is at the service of its members.

❷ FC Barcelona plays the most attractive football:
- ▶ An offensive pattern of play.
- ▶ It knows how to win and how to lose (fair play).
- ▶ Teams formed mostly of home-grown talent complemented by world-class players.

❺ Implementation. Proper usage of positioning is arguably more important than the route taken to select it. It's no point having a written, framed positioning if it is not then taken into account in the daily running of the sports property. So we need to ask ourselves if the decisions we are taking are aligned with our positioning and to use it as a source of inspiration. Let's look at some examples of decisions which will be influenced by the positioning that has been chosen or where we might simply find the opportunity to highlight it:
- ▶ Design of all the emblems that form part of the brand (trophy, badges, shirts and any other logo).
- ▶ Signing of the manager and players.
- ▶ Decisions on ticket and season ticket prices.

▸ Selection of sponsors and validation of their advertising campaigns that use the sports property's emblems.

▸ Promotional tour destinations and schedule of activities during these tours.

▸ Design of any kind of event, such as award ceremonies, presentation of new players or activities during matches.

Coach's notebook

The appeal of the chosen positioning and its natural integration into the activities of the sports property are two of the main assets that the sports marketer should exploit throughout the processes of generating media exposure, pulling in supporters and sponsors, selling and marketing; in other words, at every stage on the road to where the money is.

So now we have positioning. An important milestone on the sports marketer's roadmap and a time investment that, fortunately, will not have to be repeated that often, at least in relation to the same sports property. You should only have to re-evaluate the positioning when there are changes or turning points in the life of a sports property, such as:

▸ The arrival of new owners.
▸ Expansion into new markets.
▸ Implementation of a change in strategy.
▸ Achievement of a major sporting success for the first time ever.

From the positioning to the brand

The final section in the strategy phase of the roadmap should take us from the theoretical and intangible to the practical and tangible. We are now getting ready to transform the positioning into a brand and a business plan. Let's begin with the brand.

History and positioning, as well as the results of sport, commercial and operational management, make up what we might call the 'intangible image' of a sports property. As well as the decisions that have to be taken on the sporting and commercial level, of which we've already seen some examples, there are some fortuitous or day-to-day circumstances that will also have a decisive impact on the image of the sports property and on which the sports marketer will have little or no influence. On-the-pitch circumstances that may arise, an improvement of on the pitch results, the off-pitch actions of footballers, the way executives manage and the activities of owners in other businesses or in their private lives are all examples of situations which, depending on their recurrence and media coverage, may influence the 'intangible image'. We can see the process in the illustration below.

BRAND COMPONENTS

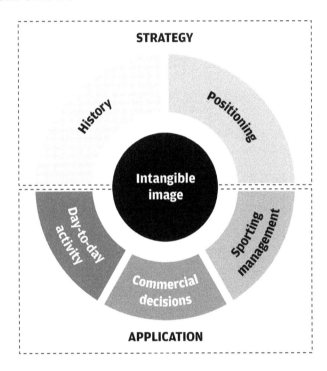

The challenge for the sports marketer is to find a way of bringing together these disparate elements under a brand.

Branding

A set of distinguishing elements that can be registered (such as name, designs, signs and symbols) and that serve to identify a sports property's products and services in the marketplace.

We can classify the distinguishing elements of a brand into four categories:

❶ **Iconography** (badge, graphic elements).

❷ **Text** (name and slogans).

❸ **Sound elements** (songs, anthems, etc.).

❹ **Informal elements** (nicknames, mascots, celebrations, rituals, chants, etc.).

In the following table, you will see some examples of distinguishing elements in the branding of different kinds of sports properties.

EXAMPLES OF DISTINGUISHING ELEMENTS

Sports property	Type	Elements	Application/examples
Champions League	Iconography Text Sound	Logo Trophy Anthem	Players' shirts, tickets, stadium advertising, merchandising. Start of match, TV screen cards.
National sides	Informal	Nicknames	The Three Lions (England), La Roja (Spain), Canarinha (Brazil), Albiceleste (Argentina), Tricolor (Mexico).
Clubs	Iconography	Badge	Official kit, merchandising.
Clubs (various)	Text	Slogans	You'll Never Walk Alone (Liverpool FC), Keep the Blue Flag Flying High (Chelsea), Marching on Together (Leeds United), More Than a Club (FC Barcelona), Hala Madrid (Real Madrid).
Clubs (various)	Informal	Nicknames	Red Devils (Manchester United), Gunners (Arsenal), Rams (Derby County), Pompey (Portsmouth), Hammers (West Ham United), Millonarios (River Plate), Las Águilas (Club América).
Footballer (various)	Iconography Text	Logo Name	Identity on social networking sites, sponsors' advertising campaigns.

Brand management

Brand management is one of the main functions of a sports marketer and their team, and it involves many tasks, including the following:

❶ Designing and renewing the iconography of existing brands.

❷ Identifying new brands and distinguishing elements that could be adopted.

❸ Legal registration to provide legal protection against potential offenders.

❹ Bestowing legitimacy upon the brand by encouraging its use by executives, technical staff and players.

❺ Getting the brand out there – using publicity in order to maximise its significance.

❻ Protecting it – monitoring its correct application by those who have the right to use it (sponsors, licensees, etc.) and prosecuting those that use it illegally or fraudulently.

During my career at FC Barcelona, I spent a lot of time and resources on tasks relating to brand management, first by taking personal responsibility for it and later by supervising the work of my team. Among the many actions that we took in relation to the FC Barcelona brand, I'd like to highlight the following:

▶ We rolled out a new corporate image (including a significant updating of the badge) and we monitored its correct use by sponsors, licensees and the media. Even today, years after leaving the club, whenever I see that a TV station or newspaper refers to FC Barcelona and shows the old badge, I'm tempted to ring up the media organisation in question or notify the club's marketing department.

▶ We developed a new brand registration policy with a new strategy based around geographical areas and product categories. The club had several registered brands besides 'FC Barcelona', such as 'Camp Nou' and 'Blaugrana' (a nickname that refers to the blue and maroon colours of the kit). We had to decide in which countries we needed to register (or renew) which brands and in which product categories (particularly important when managing merchandising licences). I recall interminable meetings with lawyers and with Patricia Plasencia, who was the club's brand manager, in which I discovered countries I'd never heard of in my entire life.

▸ We created and registered a new brand, the 'Barça Toons', a cartoon version of all the players in the first team. We started using them to promote match attendance and they ended up having their own range of merchandise. In order to increase its dissemination and legitimacy as a club brand, we started the tradition of giving every new player his own Barça Toon at every presentation press conference.

Although brand management tasks do not have an immediate impact on a sports property's revenue (as one can see from the examples given above), the sports marketer should consider them a top priority, because of how they help to create the sports property's own personalised identity, which will be converted into cash further down the line.

The brand and its distinguishing elements should be ...

▸ Unique and original. Not to be confused with other brands, and able to be legally registered.
▸ Simple. Any text must be easy to pronounce and remember.
▸ Practical. Designs should not have too many colours or graphic details that make them difficult or expensive to reproduce.
▸ Flexible. Adaptable to new product categories within the same main brand.
▸ Lasting. They should be designed so as to not become obsolete too soon.

According to *Forbes* magazine, the New York Yankees (baseball) are the most valuable sports property in the world, with a brand valued at $363 million. The global top ten, as seen in the following chart, includes five European football clubs, led by Manchester United (valued at $293 million), with Real Madrid coming in just behind it.

RANKING OF THE MOST VALUABLE SPORTS PROPERTIES IN THE WORLD

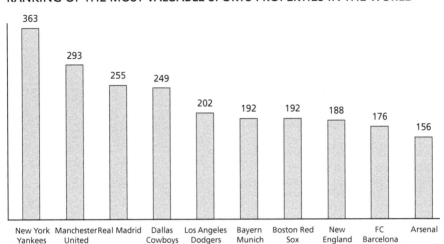

Source: Forbes, 2012
Figures in millions of US dollars.

Let's conclude this section by analysing the factors that influence a sports property's potential to generate brand value. I've divided them into four main groups:

❶ **Structural factors.** These are related to the home city or geographical area. So, the larger the economic potential and number of inhabitants in the domestic market, the greater the sports property's value potential will be. Another decisive factor that influences the value is the number of sports properties within the same geographical area, both of the same sport and of others. For example, London has five football teams usually in the Premier League (Chelsea, Arsenal, Tottenham, Fulham and West Ham), while cities such as Manchester, Liverpool, Milan, Madrid and Barcelona only have two.

❷ **Sporting success.** The trophy collection and recent sporting results, on both the collective and individual level (this need to succeed obviously does not apply to sports properties that fall into the 'tournaments and championships' category). If you're a failing side you can't expect to make as much money as if you're on the up.

❸ **Assets.** The stadium is of a far greater value if owned and not shared with other sports properties. Legendary figures – such as Pelé for Santos or Franz Beckenbauer for Bayern Munich – are also marketable. The number and passion of your season ticket holders or members is also a huge asset.

❹ **Marketing.** The accessibility of a global audience, your ability to position brand and police a wider geographical area.

Validate your decisions

By now you will have spent a huge amount of time in developing the positioning and the brand, but there is still one final step: validation of the decisions that you are about to take and implement. This is all about making sure that you do not make any catastrophic mistakes, especially when it comes to choosing the positioning and the distinguishing elements that will take you to the money. How do you do this? The key is to now ask for the views of clients and consumers (season ticket holders, supporters, current and potential sponsors, and so on). The aim is to confirm, on the one hand, whether your choice is of any relevance and, on the other, to check whether it gets positive acceptance. You may even want to ask people to choose between two or more options. Basically, now is the time for an opinion poll or some market research.

To carry this out, ideally commission a specialist company that, through interviews or telephone calls to a large number of consumers (we're talking at least in the hundreds to obtain a representative sample), will produce a comprehensive report with the answers to all our questions and concerns. However, financial limitations and the owners' relative unwillingness to invest money in such reports will, in most cases, from my experience, create a need to find alternative, cheaper or even free solutions. In this scenario, the sports marketer will have to develop a low-cost research plan and get results a different way – through questions on social networking sites and informal conversations with fans, journalists and sponsors.

Regardless of the resources available and the level of sophistication used, remember that the job of choosing and modifying the positioning of our sports property (and its distinguishing elements) cannot be considered finished until you have asked for a second opinion.

The business plan

One of the most complicated tasks for any sports marketer is to put in writing what they think the future may hold, especially if this forecasting has to then feed into the sports property's financial planning. Nobody wants to stick their neck out in such a shifting environment and in the face of such extremely volatile demand, where future financial results tend to be linked to chance or to what may or may not happen on the pitch.

Developing a good business plan is essential in any organisation of any kind, and sports properties are no exception. The business plan, which includes the sports property's medium and long-term strategy plans, will help us, among other things, to:

▶ Set objectives and monitor how they are being met, based on predefined management metrics.
▶ Plan our financial management.
▶ Present the sports property positively to potential investors.

The sports marketer, working in a team with other representatives of the sports property and high level executives (especially the finance director) will be involved in developing the documentation that is to form the main part of the business plan and that should include the following sections, at the very least:

❶ **Sporting objectives.** Whatever the size and type of sports property (except in the case of tournaments), an ambitious but at the same time realistic challenge has to be set in the sporting arena, which will serve to calculate investments in players, manage expectations of success and also to have a 'story' – a guiding theme to share with potential sponsors and business partners. This could be one of the following – competing in Europe, remaining in the division, moving up a division, getting through a particular stage in a tournament, getting a better classification than the main rival and being the highest-scoring striker or the most successful goalkeeper – all examples of possible sporting objectives, above and beyond the need to win major titles that we will always find driving the top teams. The idea, then, is to have a definition of what sporting success *actually means* for our specific sports property; one that is appropriate to our sports property's true potential.

So the sports marketer cannot hide behind the idea that the sporting side of things is not his responsibility, or the clichéd 'success and failure are all down to chance anyway'. You need to sit down with the football director responsible and agree on the sporting objectives that the marketer can then play with commercially.

Just as in the stock exchange, over- or underestimating sports results will come back to haunt you. If you have been too optimistic, you will be creating a feeling of disappointment that will negatively affect revenue. On the other hand, if you are excessively conservative in your definition of success, you will lose opportunities to capitalise on increased demand (for example, you'll find yourself with stock shortages of licensed products).

Having said that, it is always preferable to surpass expectations than to fall short.

Once you have identified and agreed your sporting objectives you need to condense these into a phrase or set of phrases that should easily fit onto a single page. It may be out of your field of influence, but these objectives should also be used as a guideline when setting the performance-related pay of players and directors.

❷ **Business vision and goals.** We should also have a phrase or set of phrases to synthesise the main medium to long-term business goals that result from the sporting objectives. Ideally, it will include goals with specific numbers based on the management metrics we have set ourselves (commonly, financial figures). For example, at FC Barcelona we set out to reach the figure of €400 million in revenue over five years. Other goals might be to reach a certain level of profitability or to stop making losses by a certain date. There is also the possibility of including mini-goals or 'milestones', such as reaching a certain number of season ticket holders, achieving a particular number of friends on Facebook or selling a certain volume of shirts in a particular geographical area. The business vision and the challenge of reaching the goals associated with it will also act as a motivator and mobiliser both of the organisation and of the general public.

❸ **Segmentation.** This classic exercise of conventional marketing demands you plot which products you want to sell, in which geographical areas and to which target audience. This is an extremely useful planning task for organising your ideas and setting priorities. You are going to have to define both a general segmentation for the sports property itself, and other more specific ones for each type of product. For example, on the general level you might set yourself the objective of pulling in more supporters aged below 30, while on the specific level you may be segmenting the process of selling season tickets based on the supporters' ability to travel to the stadium and their purchasing power (resulting in different pricing levels for season tickets). Just like the sporting objectives and the business vision, remember you must always be able to translate the segmentation strategy into a few words or phrases.

❹ **Marketing plan.** This is a summary of all the actions planned for an entire sport season for promoting and selling the products in each of the three families (stadium, marketing and media), using our earlier terminology.

⑤ Financial plan. This includes the profit and loss forecasting and all the other financial information (for example, balance sheets, budgeting, and so forth). The work of the sports marketer will, for the finance manager at least, centre on forecasting the revenue of each of the product families as well as their direct associated costs (see point 6, below). Bearing in mind that revenue forecasts are used by finance managers to forecast the general expenditure budget of the sports property, it is common to underestimate them in order to avoid any unpleasant surprises. By way of example, despite the fact that FC Barcelona's usual sporting objective is to win important titles, during my time at the club we used to do our financial planning based on reaching the quarter-finals of the UEFA Champions League every year. Documenting the financial planning will take you from PowerPoint to Excel (or from Keynote to Numbers if you speak Apple) – as with all things financial these documents will mostly be in the form of spreadsheets.

⑥ Marketing budget. You will also need a section that will include a forecast of specific marketing costs that are necessary for you to reach the revenue objectives that you have set yourself. This should include items of expenditure such as advertising, market research, travel, commissions to agencies that bring you sponsors and the production costs of sponsorship items that are not covered by the sponsors (such as advertising panels in the press room). Regardless of the size of the sports property, and even when the available budget is small or even non-existent, you still need to put it in writing in the business plan.

⑦ Project list. Those who have had the fortune or misfortune to work with me are very familiar with my dreaded project lists. I remember how something as common as a document listing the projects in progress with a description of the status, next steps, person responsible for each task and timeline caused a major upheaval in the executive committee at FC Barcelona during my early days at the club in 2002. I had drawn up my own project list in order to report and monitor the various projects, together with the club's general manager, Javier Pérez Farguell, in our weekly meetings. To my surprise and embarrassment, Javier showed my project list at one of the executive committee meetings and asked all the directors to also, from then on, report on the status of their projects in their various departments by way of a project list. They had never used this type of document before and from that moment on it was established as an instrument for monitoring projects in every department. The project list has to be included in your department's business plan, and you should commit to updating it periodically (specifying how the projects are evolving in relation to the previous review) for follow-up meetings with managers and team members.

Preparing all the documents described above requires a great deal of administrative work that many would consider a waste of time. But I strongly believe in the need to set concrete objectives (however hard that may seem in the sports world), developing clear-headed, unemotional financial plans and putting in writing the evolution of projects and the agreements reached between members of the same sports property. Doing all this will lead to a more efficient organisation whose members are more committed to producing the work expected of them.

Let's conclude this first phase in our roadmap, maybe the most theoretical (and even tedious) part of the route to the money. And while strategy planning should be present at every stage of the road, the sports marketer does have more exciting activities ahead, full of big, new challenges.

SHOW ME THE TACTICS

1 Write down the positioning you have chosen for your sports property, and share it with the organisation and with stakeholders (sponsors, journalists, opinion leaders, etc.). Don't forget to attach the 'map' that you have used to locate your competitors.
2 Validate your positioning decision through some kind of opinion poll.
3 Identify the key brands, develop a strategy for registering them and protecting them, and identify opportunities to develop new ones.
4 Develop a business plan that will include the sports objectives, the business vision, the major goals, the segmentation, the financial plan, the sales and marketing plan, the marketing budget and the project list.

Goal assists
▶ Offer stakeholders the opportunity to take part in brainstorming before selecting the positioning, as this will increase their future commitment to it.
▶ Positioning based on sporting success is undoubtedly the most appealing, given the subject matter, and the one that creates the strongest bond. Work closely with the sports director to identify a tangible goal, where the promises can be kept season after season.
▶ Draw the positioning map with more than one line, and include other sports properties of a similar size to yours (or of the size you want to reach).

- Before selecting the positioning, try it out with examples of possible future management decisions to see how it might condition what you do and whether you can fulfil it. Don't make it official if you are not yet 100 per cent certain that it's the right one.
- In the positioning validation phase, don't present more than four or five options.
- If you don't have enough budget to hire a specialist opinion polling agency, look for alternatives, gathering information through social networking sites or your own database or contacts.
- Be courageous and think about modernising the brand (at least every five years). Be innovative but without disrespecting history.
- Apply the 20/80 rule when registering and guarding the brand. Only 20 per cent of the decisions will help you get protection in 80 per cent of the potential market.
- Put some effort into condensing the positioning, the sport objectives and the business vision into a few short words or phrases. If you can't do it, it's too complicated to sell to others.
- Put in writing all the decisions that are agreed upon with other members of the organisation in relation to the most significant projects. For example, by email, meeting minutes or updating the project list. It will serve you well when others have lapses of memory or change their minds (unfortunately very common in sports management).
- The complete business plan should not be drawn up more than once a year.
- Don't be tempted to make forecasts on the spur of the moment or on the basis of very recent sports results.

PART II

MEDIA EXPOSURE AND CRITICAL MASS

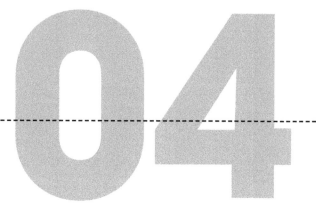

Media exposure

We have reached the second stage of our voyage and the money is still notable for its absence. However, in order to reach the commercialisation phase itself in the best condition, the sports marketer's roadmap asks us to stop and review two issues that are of massive importance on the route to the money: media exposure and critical mass.

To be or not to be in the press

If you don't yet know this you soon will do. Getting media coverage of a sports property's activities is the mother of all battles. There is no sports marketing without the press. It's that simple. The sponsors' logos may be shining bright and clear in the press room, but if they are not published in the media they are of no value: the advertising around the pitch is not directed at the people sitting in the stadium, but at the TV viewers; the presentation of a new footballer is meaningless without the presence of reporters; putting a sponsor's name to a tournament or a stadium is a complete disaster if the journalists don't use the new name in their pieces. Basically, the press multiplies the value of the content generated by a sports property exponentially, so the way it is managed must take absolute priority on the sports marketer's to-do list.

Coach's notebook

A sports property will only become significant if it achieves systematic, intensive and free presence in the media of its chosen geographical area of influence. Ideally, coverage will be in an editorial tone, positive and in a graphic format (pictures are better than words).

So from this moment on, occupying the maximum space possible in the media becomes one of the sports marketer's big obsessions. Systematic, intensive, favourable and free media presence will be a decisive factor when it comes to reaching the following objectives:

❶ Attracting supporters (critical mass).
❷ Influencing the decisions of stakeholders (sponsors, opinion leaders, etc.).
❸ Generating return on investment for sponsors (who are 'embedded' in the content).
❹ Publicising the sports property's B2C products (such as match tickets).
❺ Promoting and strengthening the chosen positioning.

How successfully you achieve these objectives will directly influence the sports property's potential to generate revenue in the commercialisation phase (the third stage on the roadmap).

Knowing the media environment

First, the sports marketer has to familiarise themselves with the most important media in the sports property's geographical area of influence (the current one or the one desired in the future) and with the way the target audience consumes sport content.

WAYS OF CONSUMING SPORT CONTENT

	USA	England	Germany	Spain	France	Italy
1	TV (96%)	TV (94%)	TV (91%)	TV (95%)	TV (91%)	TV (93%)
2	Online (56%)	Press (58%)	Press (53%)	Press (62%)	Press (45%)	Press (59%)
3	Press (53%)	Online (52%)	Online (47%)	Online (59%)	Online (45%)	Online (56%)
4	Live (51%)	Live (44%)	Radio (38%)	Radio (52%)	Live (36%)	Live (55%)
5	Radio (42%)	Radio (43%)	Live (32%)	Live (42%)	Radio (34%)	Radio (55%)

Source: Global Sports Media Consumption Report 2011 (Perform, TV Sports Markets & KantarSport)

Generally, the biggest audiences are to be found, in decreasing order, in television programmes, the written press, online media and radio stations.

The work of the sports marketer should include at the very least the following activities:

- **Segmentation:** decide which geographical area (city, region and/or country) and the profile of the target audience that we want to reach.
- **Getting audiences:** in each media organisation in general, and in specific programmes or broadcasts.
- **Classifying the media groups** based on audiences. Normally, media groups own more than one media organisation (for example, a television channel, a radio station and a newspaper), so by forging a relationship with three or four groups we should be able to concentrate most of the capacity to make an impact.
- **Identifying key journalists, presenters and opinion leaders.** These are the people who influence the programmes, broadcasts or newspaper sections with the biggest audiences. The sports marketer should set himself the objective of meeting these people and forging the best possible relationship with them.

MAIN EUROPEAN NEWSPAPERS FOR FOLLOWING SPORT NEWS

Newspaper	Country/type	Daily readership	Source / date
Bild	German General news	12,113,000	Presse II 2011
The Sun	United Kingdom General news	7,683,000	NRS July 2010–June 2011
Gazzetta dello Sport	Italy Sport	4,051,000	Audipresse April–July 2011
Marca	Spain Sport	3,011,000	EGM November 2012
L'Équipe	France Sport	2,347,000	Audipresse 2010

MAIN MEDIA ORGANISATIONS IN SPAIN

Medium	Type	Audience	Property
Tele 5	TV	17.9%	Mediaset
Marca	Press	3,011,000 readers a day	Unidad Editorial
Marca.com	Online	4,604,000 unique visitors (30 days)	Unidad Editorial
Cadena Ser	Radio	4,500,000 listeners a day	Grupo Prisa

Source: Estudio General de Medios (Spain), November 2012

Auditing content

The potential to generate media impact is closely linked to the amount and value of the content that is available. You now need to review the sports property's capacity to generate content, and we can divide this into four main groups of activities:

❶ **Sporting activity.** Matches and training sessions are possibly the 'purest' content there is and they are naturally the main focus of attention for the media. Elements such as style of play, goals, result uncertainty, rivalry, important matches or historic wins bring value to the content. The sports marketer has very little ability to influence this.

From my time at FC Barcelona, I have a very vivid recollection of the 0-3 win at the Santiago Bernabéu stadium in Madrid in November 2005, when Ronaldinho even managed to win the applause of the Real Madrid supporters. There could not have been any more valuable content to distribute to the world's media.

❷ **Communication activity.** This includes all the activities organised by the sports property where the ultimate purpose is to get media presence, such as events, presentations and press conferences. Logically, the sports marketer has complete ability to influence here, because the fundamental issues such as the content of events, choice of protagonists and timing all depend on him or her.

I remember how at Barça, whenever we had to present new commercial agreements (content that is inherently uninteresting to the media), the sponsors always wanted the club president to take part, in order to achieve greater impact. Besides the fact that the president's presence was normally linked to the financial dimension of the agreement, we always tried to schedule the press conferences at a time that did not compete with any sporting action, for example in the league pauses due to national team matches. This created greater chances of obtaining space in the media for our story.

❸ **Private life.** The actions of managers, coaches and players in spheres not directly related to the sports property, such as their private lives or other professional projects, are also a type of content that one must be keenly aware of. The sports marketer may have a minimal margin of influence in this area, but the reality is that the news that is generated produces collateral publicity impacts that have to be monitored. It is the players that are most affected by these situations, which are more often negative than positive.

❹ **Conventional advertising.** Advertising campaigns for the sports property's or the sponsors' products, using sports property content.

ACTIVITIES TO GENERATE CONTENT

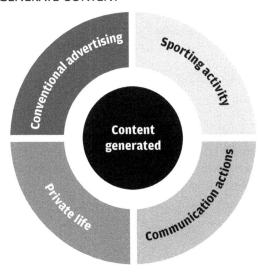

The communication plan

A sports property's communication activities are possibly the most difficult to plan, because they are exposed to constant variation, but once again it is important to write the strategy and tactics into a document. The communication plan (as the document will be called here) should include the objectives, segmentation, distribution channels, the media organisations you are prioritising and an interactive calendar of activities. Creating the documents included in the plan (which may take the form of a simple text or diagram) should not present too much work, as it does not have to be very long.

Basic structure of a communication plan

❶ **Strategic objectives.** A general description of the reasons why you want to achieve long-term media presence, such as, for example, general promotion of the sports property, giving our sponsors a return on their investment or attracting new supporters.

❷ **Tactical or short-term objectives.** These are more specific objectives that frequently change. For example, encouraging fair play, highlighting a sports result, encouraging supporters to attend matches or getting a positive evaluation of the sports property's financial management.

❸ **Geographical area.** In which city, region or country we want to achieve the media impact.

❹ **Target audience.** The segment of the population that we want to address.

❺ **Strategic media.** The groups or individual media organisations that, because of their audience, should be given special treatment.

❻ **Own channels.** If we also have our own channels (for example, a TV station, website or magazine) for distributing content.

❼ **Calendar of activities.** A table that should include all the communication events and their scheduled dates. The level of detail (for example, weekly or daily) and the frequency with which it is updated will depend on the scale of the sports property.

Distributing the content

In July 2011, to the surprise of all the journalists, the brilliant new signing for Napoli, Gökhan Inler, appeared at the press conference at which he was to be presented, wearing a lion mask: the images (along with the presence of the club's sponsors) were published all over the world. In November 2011, the president of FC Barcelona, Sandro Rosell, who is not one for giving interviews, was interviewed live by the Arabic TV station Al Jazeera to a potential audience of 60 million. In October 2011, the Real Madrid players enjoyed a go-karting race organised by Audi, one of the club's sponsors; the following day, the images made the news in both the Spanish and the international media. In March 2011, coinciding with the visit from FC Barcelona for a league match, the president of Sevilla, José María Del Nido, achieved free publicity when he gave a commemorative gift to the Barcelona players who played in the national side and won the World Cup. In November 2011, Real Madrid got free publicity in the media at their match against Osasuna at the Santiago Bernabéu, because it was the first match in their history that they had played in the morning: the Bernabéu was packed to the rafters. In October 2011, Arsenal and one of its players, Jack Wilshere, organised a Q&A session on Twitter, to answer questions from fans: this news item was covered by the traditional media, positioning the player and his club as pioneers in the use of social networks and promoting their respective Twitter accounts. To promote the big final of its star tournament, UEFA appointed Steve McManaman ambassador of the Champions League final in London 2013: in previous years they had done the same thing with Paul Breitner (Munich 2012), Gary Lineker (London 2011) and Emilio Butragueño (Madrid 2010). In September 2011, following the mistake he made in a match against Rayo Vallecano, the Real Madrid goalkeeper Iker Casillas published some of the more glaring errors of his career on his Facebook page, thereby obtaining widespread and positive coverage in the press.

These actions carried out by sports properties of various types are an illustration of some of the techniques used to achieve media exposure. To get it, one has to use the right channels for distributing content and design and execute communication events in a masterly fashion.

CONTENT DISTRIBUTION CHANNELS

Content distribution channels

1 Transfer/sale of rights

2 News coverage

3 Direct distribution

Content generated → Content published

As you can see, there are three types of **distribution channels** for disseminating content generated:

1 Transfer or sale of rights. The sports property sells or loans its broadcasting rights (mainly television) exclusively to a single channel or non-

57

exclusively to several channels. Generally speaking, as well as live match coverage, other rights are also transferred, such as the possibility of broadcasting training sessions or exclusive interviews. The audience reached will depend on the quality of the games themselves and on the profile of the channel (for example, free channels will get larger viewing figures than pay TV) and coverage is guaranteed.

❷ **News coverage.** This relates to how the media monitors the content generated by the sports property. Media presence is not guaranteed and will to a large extent depend on the design and execution of events.

❸ **Direct distribution.** Content published in the sports property's own media (magazine, website, TV channel, etc.) will reach the audience directly without any need to go through the filter of conventional media. This is also the case for those interviews or events given exclusively to a specific media organisation.

The end result, in the form of published content, will largely depend on the strategies for disseminating content and on the success of the events organisation. Let's look first at eight dissemination strategies – ways of getting our content out there – that we can put into practice, depending on the distribution channels and the type of content we are generating.

❶ **Commercial negotiation.** A process aimed at deciding on the channel and agreeing the terms and conditions for exclusive transfer or sale of TV broadcasting rights.

❷ **Lobbying.** Informal conversations with notable journalists or opinion leaders to achieve favourable publications from the content we generate (for example, positive evaluations of the team's style of play).

❸ **Design and execution.** Aspects relating to the quality of organisation of sporting and communication events. See 'How to organise a successful media event' below.

❹ **Easing access.** Make it easy for the media to access and reproduce the content that is generated (for example, access to training sessions) or granting interviews with the stars and VIPs of your sports property.

❺ **'Plug and play'.** The development and distribution of materials (such as videos, photographs or press releases) that can be reproduced by some of the media without the need for any editing.

❻ Managing bad press. Conversations with journalists and taking actions aimed at minimising the space devoted to negative news coverage and at influencing the line taken when publishing content.

❼ Buying space. The decision on which media to buy conventional advertising space for our products from. Bear in mind that it will always be easier to get news coverage in media in which you are making an advertising investment.

❽ Choosing sponsors. The advertising campaigns developed by sponsors using your content also bring free media presence for the sports property, so this factor may form part of the sponsor selection criteria (along with their financial contribution).

Below we have some examples of how dissemination strategies are applied to different types of content.

EXAMPLES OF HOW DISSEMINATION STRATEGIES ARE APPLIED

Contents	Type of activity	Distribution channels	Dissemination strategy
Matches	Sport	Transfer/sale of rights	Commercial negotiation Lobbying Design and execution
Training sessions	Sport	Transfer/sale of rights News coverage Direct distribution	Commercial negotiation Design and execution Giving access
Events	Communication	News coverage Own media	Design and execution Plug and play
Exclusive interviews	Communication	Direct distribution	Giving access
Non-sporting	Private life	News coverage	Absorption Plug and play
Products	Conventional advertising	Direct distribution	Buying ad space
Sponsors	Conventional advertising	Direct distribution	Selecting sponsors

How to organise a successful media event

❶ Invitation. Invite the media with enough advance notice and without revealing all the details of what will happen at the event.

❷ Time and date. Set the time and the date by looking for the most exclusive window possible (you do not want it to coincide with other events that are aiming to attract the same type of journalist) and with the objective of getting coverage in the TV programmes with the biggest viewing figures (news programmes).

❸ Place. Choose an iconic and original location, but one that is easy to access.

❹ Content. Carefully prepare everything that is going to happen during the course of the event. Creativity and charity-related content pull in more punters.

❺ The protagonists. Select spokespersons that are as high-ranking as possible in the organisation and include the manager and players. When it comes to the latter, plan for short sessions and situations they are comfortable in.

❻ Location of cameramen and photographers. Identify the most suitable place for television cameras and photographers by envisioning the images you want to have reproduced later on TV and in the press.

❼ Prepare the statements. Rehearse what you want to be said and think about the answers to the questions that the journalists are most likely to ask.

❽ Treatment of journalists. Provide the space and resources for the journalists to be able to do their job as comfortably as possible

❾ Materials provided. Give the journalists the pre-edited documents relating to the event (press release, pictures, etc.) so that the journalists can use them as they are and you get the content published the way you want.

❿ Sponsors and stakeholders. Identify the most prominent spaces at the venue in which to place the sponsors' logos. They should be clearly obvious, so that they later appear in the media publications in any photographs or footage.

During my time in sports marketing, I have had the opportunity to be involved in organising many communication events, and I have collected some interesting experiences and anecdotes. For example, on 5 September

2002, we organised a press conference to present the 'Gent del Barça' (Barça People) loyalty card for anyone with an affinity with the club. We did it with all due pomp, bringing in the president himself and the manager, Louis van Gaal. Although we had prepared his speech meticulously, the president, Joan Gaspart, began his talk by making reference to a controversy that was going on at the time with Real Madrid, and so inevitably this issue became the focus of attention in the following day's press, sidelining the product that we were presenting that day.

Some weeks before, we had presented an agreement that improved our sponsorship contract with Coca-Cola, one of the first contracts that I had negotiated. Ten minutes before the journalists entered, we realised that we had not produced an advertising board with Coke's logo on. Coca-Cola's marketing director mentioned that he had a sticker with the logo on, so we stuck it onto the board depicting the Barça badge that was always used in these institutional events. It looked great and the following day both logos were featured in the media behind the people who had presented the agreement. The problem arose when we tried to unpeel the sticker after the event and ruined the board, much to the fury of the great and much missed Ricard Maxenchs, the legendary assistant general manager and former general secretary, who died in 2008, having dedicated 22 years of his life to the club. The board was now good for nothing and we had to get a new one made.

It was also interesting to see, in April 2006, just before shooting an ad for Lenovo, Ronaldinho's utter joy when the executives of this Chinese computer manufacturer presented him with several laptops. I don't know if it was coincidence or not but the player was incredibly patient and engaged throughout the shoot. A few months later, we got a souvenir photo of ourselves taken in front of the Audi advertising board with my great friend and colleague Julián Fernández, after the conclusion of the media event for the release of the new cars. Without too much hassle, we got all the first team players in and media coverage the following day.

The 'non-business' of own media

When I took an interest in how the official website was going, during my first days as chief commercial and marketing officer at FC Barcelona, I was told something like 'Don't worry about it too much at the moment; it is exclusively managed by an external company that pays us good money'. It was not long before I received a call from IMG, a massive sports marketing company that was in charge of the website: 'We need to talk, Esteve,' said the project manager. IMG had an agreement with the club by which, as well as covering all the costs of producing the website, the company also paid Barça a fee. In return, IMG would keep all the revenue that it generated. As often happens, this revenue was far below their expectations and they had been losing money with us from the word go. This meant that there was a serious risk that the quality of the website would be compromised, especially in the more than likely scenario that our client would have to reduce the operating costs to improve their own accounts.

When I told the finance director that IMG wished to cancel the contract and that we should take charge of our own website, he asked me if there were any other companies that would be interested instead, adding 'How much revenue would we generate if we did it here at the club?' I told the finance director that my vision for the website was to use it as a communication tool and sales channel for the club's products, but that it would never be a business unit that, in itself, would generate profit. He was surprised at this, and asked me why I wasn't taking into account the advertising revenue. I answered that the sponsors didn't want to pay more for advertising on the website and that I didn't think it was appropriate to sell advertising space to their competitors.

This situation, as well as reminding us that if our clients do not achieve business success neither will we, arises in most sports properties, where sports marketers have to decide on which of their own media to promote and to what purpose.

The most common **own or official media** of a sports property are:

▶ The website.
▶ Publications (members' magazine, match programmes or official magazine sold at newsagents).
▶ The TV channel.
▶ Spaces on social networking sites.

During the course of my career, I have seen numerous launches of own media, but also many closures. The fact is that, before setting up a new own media channel, one must carefully study one's motives. In this sense, a sports property's own media channel should at the very least serve to:

▶ Promote the sports property in general.
▶ Communicate with the public directly.
▶ Sell your products.
▶ Offer returns to your sponsors (in the form of advertising space or the chance to sell their products).
▶ Provide services to members.
▶ Attract supporters (or 'friends' or 'followers').

As you can see, although these objectives ultimately have a commercial purpose (and therefore form part of the sports marketer's roadmap), we have not yet considered that any of your own media channels can also create business directly.

In most cases the direct costs will be greater than the revenue. So, taking into account that you have to make a financial investment, it is very important to be clear about what type of benefit you hope to obtain in return. In the following table, you can see an indication of the results you might expect from each of your own official media channels.

RESULTS WE CAN EXPECT FROM OUR OWN MEDIA CHANNEL

Objectives	Website	Publications	TV channel	Social networks
Promotion	•	•	•	•
Communication	•	•	•	•
Product sales	•	•	•	
Sponsor return	•	•	•	
Services to members	•	•		
Attract followers				•

Regardless of the decision you take when it comes to publications and the possibility of having your own TV channel (the two forms of media that have the highest associated costs), it is important to remember that the website and your presence on social networking sites are a must. One might even go so far as to say that if you don't have enough funds, social networking sites can also meet the objectives of a website.

Social networking sites

Social networking sites are a direct, immediate, informal and affordable way of communicating with your supporters in every corner of the globe. Here, we shall be focusing on YouTube, Facebook and Twitter as the social networking sites that can help you to distribute audio-visual content (as long as you have the rights to them) in a seemingly informal and improvised (but really an organised and planned) manner. For example, a YouTube channel can serve as a TV channel for a sports property with a low budget, because the space and broadcast cost nothing.

On 26 May 2013, at 2.03 a.m. UK time, Brazilian star Neymar announced in his Twitter account his signing as an FC Barcelona player, ahead of official statements by the Catalans and Santos FC (seller club). On 16 January 2013, Bayern announced the signing of Pep Guardiola as their manager as of July 2013, solely through its Twitter account. On 7 February 2011, the FC Barcelona player Gerard Piqué uploaded a photo onto his Facebook page, thereby confirming his relationship with the pop singer Shakira, and later used Twitter to confirm his girlfriend's pregnancy and present his son Milan to the world in February 2013. On 28 July 2011, Sergio 'Kun' Agüero confirmed his signing with Manchester City FC by tweeting: 'I am now a City player. Happy to be at this club and in this city. Thank you everyone for the welcome and the reception.' As you can see, the use of Facebook, Twitter and even Instagram by clubs and footballers for distributing exclusive content

Tips for maximising followers on Facebook and Twitter

▶ Exclusivity of content. Publishing exclusive news, opinions and photographs.

▶ Publishing as many events or tweets as possible.

▶ Commiting to publishing. Uploading content as regularly as possible and avoiding 'disappearing' for long periods of time. Publishing the 'bad news' too.

▶ Wherever possible, identifying the space with a single person.

▶ Remembering the significance of authenticity. It is important that the content is created by the same person that is giving it (or appearing to give it), in his or her communication style and only in the languages he or she speaks.

▶ The name of the space should be the original name of the sports property or as similar as possible to it. Trying to ensure that the official space is easily distinguished from its imitators. Twitter provides a verification service to prove an account's authenticity, which is indicated by a blue tick on the profile in question.

▶ Spending time interacting with followers and answering their questions.

▶ Offering prizes to followers in the form of items that are not readily available, such as tickets or signed shirts.

is now common practice and has forced journalists to follow the content published on social networking sites very closely. It has also democratised content, making it available to everyone without exclusivity or hindrances.

Facebook and Twitter have therefore become powerful communication tools that lies within the reach of any sports property, regardless of its size or profile. The sports marketer should therefore have a basic knowledge of how they work, and the results in the form of pulling in new followers will be a very important milestone on your route to where the money is.

PROS AND CONS OF THE BEST-KNOWN SOCIAL NETWORKING SITES

Social networking sites	Pros	Cons
YouTube	Audience Low cost Immediacy	Owned by third party No advertising revenue Unidirectional
Facebook	Immediacy Interactivity Low cost Clear message	Owned by third party No advertising revenue Imitation (fake) accounts
Twitter	Immediacy Interactivity Low cost Clear message	Owned by third party No advertising revenue Imitation (fake) accounts

From generated content to published content

In the final section of this chapter, we shall look at evaluating the results of the work we have done to generate content. They will, of course, depend only and exclusively on the content that has actually been published or reproduced in the media. So, to 'close the circle', we need to:

1 Get information on all the content published or reproduced in relation to our sports property.
2 Make an assessment based on the objectives we set.
3 Identify errors and aspects of the execution that can be improved.
4 Organise a file (actual or digital) in which to store actual samples of the content that has been published.

SHOW ME THE TACTICS

❶ Draw up a list of the main media groups, channels, programmes, publications and key journalists for your selected geographical area and audience profile.

❷ Try to identify the capacity to generate content in each category (sporting activity, communication actions, private life and conventional advertising).

❸ Review the content published about your sports property in the past (or before your arrival).

❹ Write your communication plan, and make sure that the strategic and tactical objectives fit with the positioning and have been agreed with the rest of the organisation.

❺ Decide which of your own media channels you want, and earmark a cost and revenue budget for each of them.

❻ Reserve the rights to the name of your sports property on the internet and on social networking sites.

❼ Find out what audio-visual content you have at your disposal (in other words, what has not been sold or given) and that you can distribute through social networking sites.

❽ Get the contact details of all the journalists that come to your communication events and keep them in a database.

❾ Create the file in which to store all the published content (your clippings file).

Goal assists

▶ The communication plan is strictly confidential and you should not share it with anyone outside the organisation.

▶ Update the tactical objectives and the calendar of activities in the communication plan at least once a month.

▶ Use your creativity and originality when producing content and events. Taking the events out of our everyday context (stadium or training ground) can produce very good results.

▶ Try to be proactive with journalists when trying to get your content published.

▶ Be in a constant dialogue with journalists, thanking them for their positive pieces and trying to rectify the negative ones (or the lack of pieces).

- ▶ Bear in mind that if you have a budget to invest in conventional advertising, it will be easier for you to get free coverage of your activity in the media in which you buy advertising space and harder to get in those you have not selected. So ask for free coverage of your activities as a condition for buying advertising space.
- ▶ If you want players to come to the events, organise fun activities.
- ▶ Don't try to compete with the media by exclusively using your own media. They have more experience and more resources.
- ▶ Own media channels that do not have sufficient resources can harm the image of the sports property. It's better to have none at all if you cannot guarantee a minimum level of quality and frequency of updates.
- ▶ Share the published content with the sponsors, especially if they appear in the published piece.
- ▶ Keep the positioning of your sports property at the forefront of your mind in all your decision-making.

05

In search of the critical mass

You have been hard at work, and your sports property now has a unique positioning and regularly appears in the media of your chosen geographical area. Your commercial product is almost ready, and we are getting closer and closer to the money. All that's missing is the icing on the cake: supporters, en masse. Indeed, the number of supporters is one of the main indicators of the size and importance of a sports property, so attracting and building the loyalty of as many fans as possible will also be one of the sports marketer's principal objectives in the phase leading up to commercialisation per se.

The value of the critical mass of supporters

On 7 February 2013, FC Barcelona celebrated that it had reached 40 million fans on Facebook, doubling the 20 million it had reached in September 2011; and also that the Spanish Football Federation, with more than 800,000 licences, was now the federation with the highest number of licensed sportsmen and women in Spain, doubling that of the Basketball Federation in second place.

These figures provide good examples of the kind of tools that a sports marketer would like to always have within reach. First, because they consist of big numbers (critical mass) that grow exponentially; and second, because they are a powerful and very commercially valuable database to be exploited.

Developing and maintaining as large a mass of supporters as possible translates into two major benefits for the sports property:

❶ **It adds strategic value to negotiations,** such as sponsorship projects, the sale of TV rights or corporate transactions (for example, the sale of the sports property).

RANKING OF FEDERATION LICENCES IN SPAIN

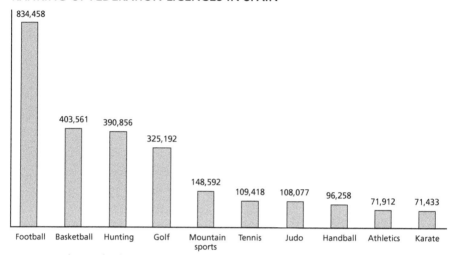

Source: Consejo Superior de Deportes 2011

❷ **It is a business opportunity in itself,** because of both the potential to sell your own products directly (for example, match tickets) and the possibility to release them to third parties through corresponding commercial agreements.

The supporter numbers kit

The process of attracting supporters requires another level of analysis from the sports marketer. The number of supporters in general is important, but their level of commitment to and affection for the sports property is also very important.

As you can see from the illustration opposite, we shall be using the level of engagement (from least to greatest) to group the fans into four main categories:

❶ **People who show interest.** People who follow tournaments, national sides, clubs or players as a form of entertainment. They may have a particular liking for a certain sports property, but without this leading to a bond of affection.

❷ **Supporters.** We refer here to the fans that, as well as showing an interest, express their preference for and emotional connection with a team or player (generally speaking, I don't believe that one has an affective relationship with a tournament).

LEVEL OF SUPPORTERS' ENGAGEMENT WITH THE SPORTS PROPERTY

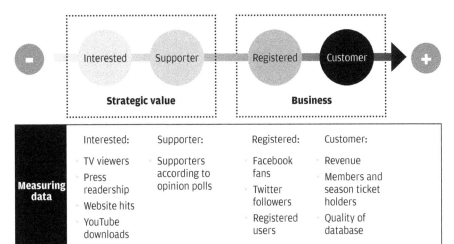

	Interested:	Supporter:	Registered:	Customer:
Measuring data	TV viewers Press readership Website hits YouTube downloads	Supporters according to opinion polls	Facebook fans Twitter followers Registered users	Revenue Members and season ticket holders Quality of database

❸ **Registered users.** The next level of engagement is found when supporters go one step further and provide their details when registering on one of the sports property's own media channels, be it the website, a newsletter, Facebook or Twitter. It is in this sphere that the opportunity arises for you to communicate directly with supporters registered to these channels.

❹ **Customers.** This is the group with the highest level of commitment, as they also have a monetary relationship with the sports property. These are supporters that periodically pay for a product or service (such as a member's card or a season ticket) or that have at some point bought a product and provided their details (for example, a ticket or an official shirt) and agree to then be contacted to receive information on other offers.

It is clear, then, that the sports marketer's objective is to get as many customers as possible, but without forgetting that the followers on the lower levels of engagement are also of great value.

Coach's notebook

Developing a critical mass of supporters that is large, measurable, demonstrable and sustainable over time greatly helps to generate commercial value for a sports property.

RANKING OF CLUBS BY NUMBER OF SUPPORTERS IN EUROPE

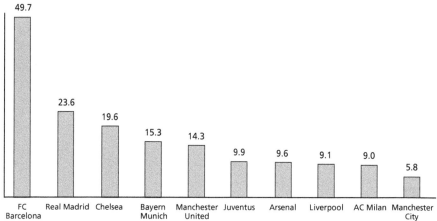

Source: Sport+Markt 2012
Figures in millions of supporters

The *Fan Survey*, produced by the German consultancy Sport+Markt (now rebranded as Repucom) and published in late 2012, indicated that FC Barcelona, with 49.7 million supporters, was by far the most popular club in Europe.

I well remember that during my time at FC Barcelona, we started buying this study, which comes out annually, on a regular basis to use it as one of the principal indicators of the result of our supporter recruitment drive. We were interested in both the absolute number of supporters and in the difference with our main rivals, Real Madrid and Manchester United. In fact, in my last complete season at the club (2006–07), we had the pleasure of celebrating the fact that Sport+Markt's *Fan Survey* stated that we had at last managed to overtake Real Madrid in supporter numbers. Undoubtedly, the UEFA Champions League title won in Paris in May 2006 had a lot to do with it.

One could say that the almost 50 million supporters illustrated in the *Fan Survey 2012*, together with the 40 million fans on Facebook (registered supporters) and the 175,000 members (customers), make up FC Barcelona's 'supporter numbers kit' (and what a fantastic kit), which should be used to add value in the commercialisation phase.

Every sports marketer should have his or her own numbers kit (including the number of 'people who show interest', 'supporters', 'registered users' and 'customers') for their sports property, regardless of whether these numbers are in the millions, thousands or hundreds. For example, as we can see below, the numbers of Facebook fans of clubs in the Spanish Second

FACEBOOK FANS OF SPANISH 2ND DIVISION CLUBS 2012/13

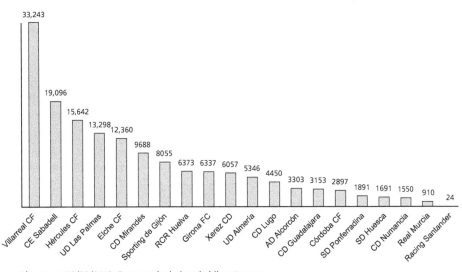

Figures on 12/02/2013. Does not include subsidiary teams.

Division in the 2012/13 season are much more modest, but they still form part of the numbers kit of each and every team (with some major 'catch-up work' to be done by some sports marketers).

The 'pulling in the punters' mindset

The tasks that a sports marketer must carry out to pull in the supporters are not necessarily the most impactful in the short term. There are a number of factors that have a decisive influence on the result, and over which you have very little or no influence at all. Nevertheless, as a sports marketer, you should have the goal of attracting new supporters in your mind at all times and this should be reflected in every decision you make during the working day.

Above and beyond the mentality that we, as sports marketers, should develop, of always 'pulling in the punters', we can also identify three types of factors or activities that will have a decisive influence on the scale and growth of supporter numbers: (1) historical and structural; (2) strategic and sports management; and (3) product sales activities.

❶ **Historical and structural factors.** The Argentine national football team is one of the most popular in the world, undoubtedly because of the quality of its players but, more than that, because of its past sporting successes. It has an enviable trophy cabinet, with two World Cups and 14 Copa América victories. Despite the fact that it won its last World

Cup more than 25 years ago (Mexico 1986) and its last Copa América in 1993 (in Ecuador), the Argentine national side is still one of the teams with the most supporters in the world. The same applies to Arsenal, which won three Premier League titles and four FA Cups between 1998 and 2005 but has since been without silverware. Football has also enjoyed the magic of 'one and only' players such as Pelé, Maradona, Cruyff and Zidane and, more recently, Messi and Cristiano Ronaldo. These examples serve to illustrate how past sporting successes and the presence of exceptional footballers, among other factors we shall see below, help to pull in supporters. These are all factors over which the sports marketer can have little influence and from which the results (in terms of supporter recruitment) will come in the medium to long term.

❷ **Strategic and sports management.** Neymar, a player with Santos in Brazil, is now among the most popular footballers in the world, despite being aged just 21 and never having played for a European team. He has achieved this, as well as through his unquestionable technical skill, because of the excellent work of the sports marketers that advise him. Their 'pull in the punters' mindset is second to none, and they have been masterly in the way they have managed his positioning, media exposure and the advertising campaigns of his sponsors. We can also see how the signing of certain players to a football club can really help to bring in followers in certain geographical areas. For example, the signing of former Real Madrid player Raúl helped German team Schalke 04 to win supporters in Spain, and the signing of Chicharito Hernández did the same for Manchester United in Mexico. Although the sporting decisions aren't the direct responsibility of the sports marketer (even though you may, of course, be consulted), appropriate decisions on positioning, good segmentation of the audience you want to reach and achieving recurrent media exposure, among other things, are a vital part of your everyday work and will have a strong impact on supporter recruitment in the short to medium term.

❸ **Product sales.** The tasks that have the most immediate and visible impact are those relating to the distribution of the sports property's own online media and products and those of its strategic partners. The most common media or products are the website (with a registration process for certain exclusive areas or the newsletter), official spaces on social networks, membership cards and season tickets. The sponsors' products (for example, the sports property's official credit card marketed by your banking industry sponsor) can also provide interesting numerical data that you can include in our kit.

The sports marketer should therefore concentrate on strategic management and on commercialisation to maximise the impact when developing a critical mass of supporters. But all this must be done without forgetting that the 'pull in the punters' mindset must accompany each and every decision you make.

THE IMPACT OF ACTIVITIES THAT CAN INFLUENCE SUPPORTER RECRUITMENT

	Historical/structural	Strategic and sports management	Product commercialisation
Factors/ actions	• Sporting successes (historically) • Family tradition • Strength of local market • Exceptional footballers • Work of previous managers	• Sporting success (recent) • Selection and observance of positioning • Media exposure • Line-up of players (clubs) • Sponsors' campaigns • Target audience segmentation	• Premium space on website • Spaces on social networks • Membership or fan card • Season tickets • Third party products
Ability to influence	*	***	*****
Immediacy of results	*	***	*****

He who has a database is wealthy beyond words

So you're beginning to build a strong picture of supporter numbers, partly through your own gathered data of interested people and followers, partly through a number of direct businesses, and partly through the numbers your registered users and customers create for you.

The next step involves concentrating on developing and maintaining a powerful database in which to store the information you have on registered supporters and current or past customers. The capacity of this database to generate business and become a useful communication tool will largely depend on its quality.

The sports marketer's goal is to develop a database with the greatest possible number of registered users (or supporters or customers) and the largest possible amount of information on each of them. This objective is a fundamental part of the 'pulling in the punters' mindset, so the sports marketer should bear in mind that many of your decisions and daily activities can help to increase the number of entries in his database.

To do so, you need to concentrate essentially on three types of activities: (1) recruitment; (2) conversion; and (3) maintenance.

❶ **Recruitment actions.** Actions designed to add completely new entries to your database. The daily life of a sports property offers numerous opportunities to obtain useful entries without having to incur significant additional costs. Let's look at some different options:
  ▶ Asking for the details (even if it's just an email address) of sporadic buyers of the sports property's B2C products, such as tickets and licensed products.
  ▶ Requesting the databases that sponsors may have created with their own campaigns to recruit our supporters.
  ▶ Organising special promotions through the website or social networks.
  ▶ Reaching agreements with special groups such as fan clubs or associations so that they provide their members' details.

❷ **Conversion actions.** The goal here is to improve the quality of entries that you already have. Use the basic data that exist (such as email addresses) to obtain more detailed information on the supporter, such as their full name, age, location, etc. Constructing a special promotion that can only be accessed by plugging in personal details can be a useful way to get this information.

❸ **Maintenance actions.** Interactions with 'signed up' supporters will help you to increase their degree of loyalty and satisfaction, but also to keep their details updated. By simply answering supporters' questions, you can achieve very good results. Asking supporters for their views on current goings-on creates a feeling of belonging and consultation.

In all your activities relating to recruitment, conversion and database records maintenance, it is crucial to obtain the supporters' consent before sending them notifications. It is also very important to give them the chance to cancel their registration at any time. To this end, it is vital that the sports marketer be very familiar with the current legislation in the relevant geographical area.

The ideal database ...

❶ Has a variety of fields for each entry. The more data you have on your supporters, the more commercially valuable the database will be, as you will be able to segment it (for example, communications sent to people of a certain age group, occupation or location).

❷ Is made up of useful entries. Let's not forget that the basis for each entry is the supporter's emotional connection to the sports property. Supporters who do not meet this requirement should not be included in the database.

❸ Has up-to-date data. Supporters' details change frequently, so the goal is to find out about these changes as much as possible.

❹ Is supported by the right technology. You must be able to access it easily, edit it and segment it.

❺ Facilitates communication. It allows supporters to communicate with the sports properly through the forms of contact provided (normally by email or phone).

❻ Stores information on supporter participation. It includes information on queries they have made and, ideally, on their purchasing history.

❼ Is legal. The data have been gathered by complying with current legislation.

❽ Can be accessed by just a few people. The information contained in the database is extremely confidential and subject to important legal requirements, so the fewer people that have access to it, the better.

I have a vivid memory of when, in 2003, the vice-president Ferran Soriano suggested that we clean up the database of Barça members. We knew that many of their details were incorrect, that some membership cards were being used fraudulently and even that some members in the database had passed away some time ago. At one board meeting, Ferran proclaimed: 'We shall track each member down one by one, we shall update all their details and we shall even take a picture of them to put on the membership cards.' It seemed like mission impossible, given that we were talking of no fewer than 105,000 members at that point. However, with Ferran's determination, a huge group effort and the allocation of all the resources that were needed, the objective was achieved in just a few short weeks. The result was a database with more than 100,000 entries (today, it has more than 175,000 entries), with a variety of fields (full name, exact address and age of each member and contact details), guarded by the best imaginable watchman, the legendary Félix Palau, a great friend and, if my calculations are correct, the longest-serving employee at the club, with more than 30 years of devoted service.

We now have a commercial product

Developing a critical mass of supporters completes the most strategic work on the sports marketer's roadmap. Together with all the other elements we've looked at so far (positioning, brands and media exposure), it will turn into what we shall call the sports property's 'commercial product', that we need to respect and use in the phase that is about to begin: the marketing of all the different products.

THE COMMERCIAL PRODUCT

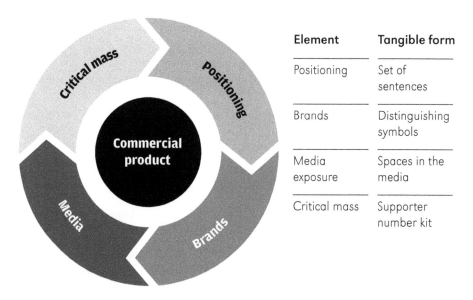

Element	Tangible form
Positioning	Set of sentences
Brands	Distinguishing symbols
Media exposure	Spaces in the media
Critical mass	Supporter number kit

And now, let's go after that money!

SHOW ME THE TACTICS

❶ Set your supporter recruitment objectives in numbers, with a specific period of time and for strategically chosen segments (for instance focusing on the right target audience and geographical areas).

❷ Assemble your supporter numbers kit, deciding which data to include and analysing its evolution over time.

❸ Identify the sources of information that you will use to measure the results.

❹ Find out about the databases that are already available at your sports property.

❺ Decide what your supporter database will look like, including the technology you will use, the data fields you want for each entry and the communication channels (Twitter, email, phone) and frequency of interaction with supporters.

❻ Check that the database meets all the legal requirements.

Goal assists

▶ Set out 'milestones' along the way to your supporter recruitment target, with numbers that can be achieved in short time frames.

▶ Try to have some influence or involvement in any sporting decisions that may influence your work, for example signing a new player to the team. Faced with the choice of two players that both meet the technical requirements, the one that may have the biggest impact on your supporter recruitment targets will be much more useful to you.

▶ Try and figure out your rival's numbers kits, to act as a comparison with the data that you have in yours.

▶ Use any positive data commercially (for example, data relating to your competitors or the growth of your fan base).

▶ Even if you don't have the budget available for commissioning reports on supporter numbers produced by specialist companies, identify and use alternative, free sources of information (such as social networking data, published TV viewing figures and hits on your official website).

▶ Celebrate and communicate your big recruitment milestones (for example, reaching a round figure of Facebook fans).

▶ It is important to maximise entries in your database, but not at any price.

> ▶ Get into the frame of mind of also getting entries for the database through the day-to-day running of the sports property.
>
> ▶ Remember to include all the required legal notices wherever you collect supporters' personal details, so that you can then exploit the database freely and legally without any restrictions.
>
> ▶ When you are communicating directly with supporters, try to achieve a good balance. Too many notifications are irritating and not enough make it hard to build their loyalty. Do not leave customers' questions unanswered.
>
> ▶ Carefully review the four parts that make up the 'commercial product' and make sure that you are happy with their contents.
>
> ▶ Keep the positioning of your sports property at the forefront of your mind in all your decision-making.

PART III

SALES

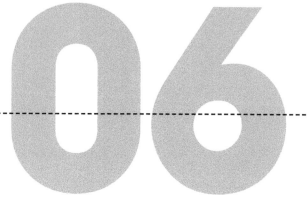

Packing the stadium

Selling. That's what it's all about at the end of the day. The roadmap is clear: we have come to the selling phase and the money is just around the corner. And we shall start to look for it by selling our own events (usually matches); the most traditional stream of income for most sports properties.

Managing to fill a stadium week after week has become a massive challenge for any sports marketer in this day and age. The financial crisis, the aging stadia, TV broadcasts (be they free or at ever more affordable prices and with better technology) and the excessive number of matches, among other factors, have led to a gradual decline in the number of spectators who come to see live matches. A general sense of pessimism has been spreading around the world of football. As an example, Italian Serie A (as you can see in the diagram overleaf) has seen a fall in season ticket sales that coincides with the spectacular growth of audiences of the pay-TV channels that bought the broadcasting rights.

On top of that, if our sports property's team is not performing on the pitch to the expected level, or if it has no important sporting objectives, the challenge is even greater.

But despite all this, the sports marketer can still have a decisive influence on attendance and on the revenue generated though match sales, so don't sit back and relax when adverse circumstances inevitably arise. On the contrary, with the right frame of mind and effective management, you can achieve some very positive results.

Crowd attendance and the multiplier effect

We shall not spend time here exploring the direct impact that spectator attendance at the stadium has on revenue. We all know that the greater the attendance, the greater the ticket sales and the more fans will spend during the matches. But direct revenue is just one of the major benefits that high attendance figures bring.

EVOLUTION OF SEASON TICKET HOLDERS VS PAY-TV AUDIENCES FOR THE ITALIAN SERIE A

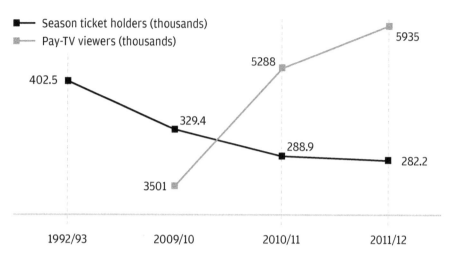

- ■ Season ticket holders (thousands)
- ■ Pay-TV viewers (thousands)

402.5

329.4

5288

288.9

5935

3501

282.2

| 1992/93 | 2009/10 | 2010/11 | 2011/12 |

Source: La Gazzetta dello Sport

ATTENDANCE AND THE MULTIPLIER EFFECT

Mass attendance

Better event

More revenue per match

Players more motivated to win

More valuable TV rights

More interested sponsors

A sell-out stadium, full, match after match, brings many advantages, including:

▸ **More chance of winning matches,** because players are more motivated if the stadium is packed to the rafters. The atmosphere this creates also helps fans to be livelier during the match.
▸ **Greater value of the TV product.** The spectacle is visually much more attractive, so the TV audiences will be bigger and, generally, there will be more channels interested in buying the rights, and probably at a higher price.
▸ **More potential sponsors** given the opportunity to associate their image with successful events, and, with a larger audience, a greater advertising imapct.

Let's look at a ranking of the main European leagues arranged in order of stadium attendance and showing their commercial revenue.

SPECTATOR ATTENDANCE VS COMMERCIAL REVENUE IN THE MAJOR EUROPEAN LEAGUES

League	Stadium occupation 2011/12	Average attendance 2011/12	Commercial revenue 2011/12
Bundesliga (Germany)	96.3%	44,293	885
Premier (England)	88.6%	34,646	772
La Liga (Spain)	66.8%	26,050	543
Serie A (Italy)	62.0%	22,005	447
Ligue 1 (France)	65.8%	18,869	399

Source: Prime Time Sport (occupation and attendance) and Deloitte (commercial revenue and sponsorship)

Revenue figures in millions of euros

The scorecard of factors influencing match attendance

▶ On 15 May 2011, the Spanish team Getafe, from the outskirts of Madrid, was playing to remain in the first division of the Spanish La Liga in a life-or-death duel against Pamplona's Osasuna, and it did not manage to fill the stadium, assembling only 13,500 spectators at the Coliseum Alfonso Pérez (which has a seating capacity of 17,700).

▶ In the summer of 2011, the new Qatari owners of Paris Saint-Germain spent €87 million on player signings and saw the club membership go from 7,000 to 20,000 in the 2011/12 season.

▶ In the '*clásicos*' (FC Barcelona vs Real Madrid), the 'sold out' sign goes up, every time.

▶ In Spain, it is common for lower division leagues to schedule their competition matches on bank holidays so that they do not need to compete with the elite matches. That way, they can get more bums on seats and more coverage in the media.

These four real situations all reflect different scenarios that the sports marketer will have to face. For example, the directors of Getafe face huge competition from the two big Madrid teams (Real Madrid and Atlético Madrid) and very little tradition of fans coming to the stadium in big numbers. However hard the sports marketer tries, it will always be difficult to fill the stadium. In the case of Paris Saint-Germain, the sports marketer will be rubbing his hands with glee because, almost without lifting a finger, they will be able to sell much more appealing matches. When it comes to the Real Madrid vs FC Barcelona *clásicos*, their respective sports marketers (of which I was fortunate to be one) can hardly claim the credit for filling the stadia. Finally, sports properties in which directors are able to decide on the match calendar and times have at their disposal one of the most powerful tools for influencing attendance results, as we shall see below.

Good crowd sizes at stadia depend on a range of different factors, on which the sports marketer will not always have decision-making power. I have identified a total of 23 factors, which can be grouped into four main categories: (1) structural; (2) sporting; (3) match day; and (4) management.

❶ Structural factors. These are the factors that are subject to minimal changes over time or that change infrequently. With the exception of the stadium, the sports marketer has zero ability to make changes.

- ▶ **Tradition.** Whether there is a custom of seeing matches live or not.
- ▶ **Purchasing power** of potential spectators.
- ▶ **Competition.** Whether there are other sports properties in the same city (or nearby) or not.
- ▶ **Population numbers.** The number of inhabitants of the geographical area of influence.
- ▶ **Stadium** in which the matches will be held (if there is a home ground).

❷ Sporting factors.

- ▶ **Sporting success.** The momentum of good results in the form of titles, winning streaks or specific milestones.
- ▶ **Quality of the squad.** The performance given on the pitch in terms of the players' technical skills and style of play.
- ▶ **Special players.** If star players are taking part or not.

❸ Match day. This category encompasses all the situations that converge around a specific match.

- ▶ **Importance of the result.** If the match is decisive (for example if there is the chance of being eliminated from a tournament) or if there is the chance to rectify a poor result.
- ▶ **Uncertainty of the result.** The difficulty of predicting the winner will create increased interest in the match (and vice versa where the result is pretty much a foregone conclusion).
- ▶ **Good or bad form** that the teams are in.
- ▶ **Rivalry.** When there is a tradition of intense rivalry between the two teams, such as the classic derby matches between Liverpool and Everton, Manchester United and Manchester City, or Chelsea and Arsenal.
- ▶ **Competition.** If there are other entertainment events scheduled in the same area or on TV at the same time.
- ▶ **The weather.** Bad weather always discourages all but the most hardy supporters from coming to the ground. This is one of the sports marketer's worst enemies.

- ▶ **News of the day,** such as the first match of a new signing, the chance of beating a goal record or the return of an important player after a long absence.
- ▶ **Chance and technical circumstances** that may lead to the absence of key players such as injuries, manager decisions or match bans.

❹ **Management.** This is where the sports marketer's ability to influence attendance is concentrated and includes:

- ▶ **The fixtures calendar,** particularly in relation to anticipating availability and the dates of the most important fixtures. A sports marketer has influence here when they're working for a league or tournament, rather than for a club (this also applies to 'Time and day' and 'Competition format' below).
- ▶ **Day and time** scheduled for matches.
- ▶ **Competition format.** Number of matches and participating teams, group stage versus play-off, etc.
- ▶ **Non-sport content.** Activities aimed at optimising the supporters' entertainment experience of a specific match, such as half-time entertainment.
- ▶ **Ticket price** (single and season tickets).
- ▶ **TV broadcasts.** As well as adverse weather conditions, live television broadcasts are the sports marketer's main adversary when it comes to filling the stadium.
- ▶ **Communication.** Conventional advertising and activities aimed at achieving news coverage in the media prior to the match.

The table opposite should help us to identify the factors that have the greatest influence on attendance and that can most easily be influenced by the sports marketer.

As you can see from the scorecard, it is the factors relating to match day that have the greatest influence on attendance results – whether it's a strong rival you're playing, whether the result is likely to be a close-fought thing – whether your key player is off the bench for the first time in a while. But it is these factors, along with the structural and sporting factors, on which the sports marketer has the least influence, and together they make up around two-thirds of the potential impact. Therefore, it is the factors relating to management, over which you, as the sports marketer, should have complete control and responsibility, that should be the focus of attention for your work, even if they cannot make the biggest impact on the attendance numbers at the ground.

As a sports marketer you need to get used to living with a wide range of circumstances that have a decisive impact on the management and results

----

SCORECARD OF FACTORS INFLUENCING MATCH ATTENDANCE

Category / importance	Factor	Score	Sports marketer's influence
Structural 10–15%	Tradition	★☆☆☆☆	☆☆☆☆☆
	Purchasing power	★★☆☆☆	☆☆☆☆☆
	Competition	★★☆☆☆	☆☆☆☆☆
	Local population	★★☆☆☆	☆☆☆☆☆
	Stadium	★★★★★	★★☆☆☆
Sporting 15–20%	Sporting success	★★★★★	★☆☆☆☆
	Quality of squad	★★★★★	★☆☆☆☆
	Special players	★★★☆☆	★☆☆☆☆
Match day 35–40%	Importance of result	★★★★★	☆☆☆☆☆
	Uncertainty of result	★★★☆☆	☆☆☆☆☆
	Form	★★★★★	☆☆☆☆☆
	Rivalry	★★★★★	☆☆☆☆☆
	Competition	★★★☆☆	☆☆☆☆☆
	The day's news	★★★☆☆	☆☆☆☆☆
	Weather	★★★★★	☆☆☆☆☆
	Fortuitous circumstances	★★★☆☆	☆☆☆☆☆
Management 30–35%	Fixtures calendar[1]	★★★☆☆	★★☆☆☆
	Day and time[1]	★★★★★	★★☆☆☆
	Competition format[1]	★★☆☆☆	★★☆☆☆
	Non-sporting content	★☆☆☆☆	★★★★★
	Price	★★☆☆☆	★★★★★
	TV broadcast[2]	★★★★★	★☆☆☆☆
	Communication	★★★☆☆	★★★★★

[1] Maximum ability to influence if sports marketers are working for tournaments.
[2] If the TV rights have been sold or transferred beforehand.

of your sports property and where you will have very little or no ability to influence or intervene.

What you have to do, then, is to concentrate your efforts on those activities that you can influence.

The exploitation of the stadium diagram

So, you want to increase spectator numbers and capitalise on the way the stadium is used. There are five main areas to organise to achieve this. By effectively managing all of them, you can maximise the chance of continued success when it comes to attendance and sales. The five areas to organise are:

❶ **Event.** Everything that relates to the match itself – the teams that are playing, the form they are in and the fixtures calendar.

❷ **Stadium.** The decisions that have to do with the venue in which the matches will take place – home, away or neutral.

❸ **Products.** Decision-making on the products to be sold, based on predicted attendance. You should focus mainly on season tickets and single ticket sales, bearing in mind the different groups of potential buyers.

❹ **Experience.** This encompasses all the interactions that take place between the spectator and the sports property before, during and after matches and which together create an evaluation of the whole experience.

❺ **Sales and marketing.** This refers to the commercial management per se, where most of the sports marketer's work will be concentrated.

THE DIAGRAM FOR COMMERCIAL EXPLOITATION OF THE STADIUM

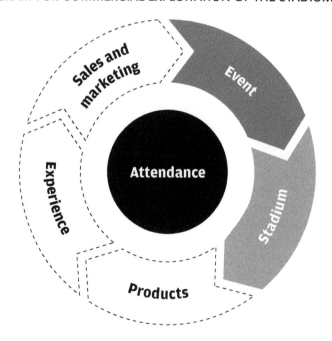

The content of events

Although many of us as sports marketers would love to have the power to make decisions on signings, be managers or even get a kit on and start playing, the fact is that when it comes to the content of games (the first block in the diagram on commercial exploitation of the stadium) we have to accept that our capacity to influence is pretty limited. The appeal of the events is mostly linked to factors of a sporting nature. Even so, the sports marketer can have a say, to a greater or lesser extent, in the decisions on:

❶ The dates and times of fixtures, except where clubs and/or national sides give this decision-making power to tournament organisers or the TV stations that have bought the broadcasting rights.

❷ The non-sport content in the form of planned additional entertainment before and/or after matches.

The truth is that my experience at FC Barcelona, when it came to producing entertainment around the games, was not an entirely positive one. For example, when, in the 2003/04 season, the team had to compete in the UEFA Cup (now the Europa League) when it was more used to being in the Champions League, we decided to hold a marketing campaign to attract spectators to the ground. Under the slogan *'Camí a Göteborg'* (Road to Gothenburg, the city that was to host the final), we arranged various activities to promote the matches, including entertainment before kick-off. The results could hardly have been more discouraging. Faced with smaller-scale rivals and ties virtually decided in the first match, at the matches against the Bulgarian side, Matador Púchov, the Greek Panionios and the Danish Brøndby, we only managed to pull in 30,000, 25,000 and 46,000 fans respectively (the stadium has seating capacity for 99,000 spectators). But for the match against Celtic, a stronger rival, and having lost the first match away 1-0, with the very same marketing actions we brought 74,000 people into the Camp Nou. Our disappointing promotional campaign was put out of its misery when we were eliminated by the Scottish team.

During that same season, we set ourselves the objective of increasing the amount of time fans would spend in the Camp Nou on match days. Unlike in other countries, the fans of FC Barcelona are in the habit of arriving at the stadium just before kick-off. We wanted to get spectators to come to the ground earlier and thereby increase their spending in cafés, restaurants and official stores, and also avoid bottlenecked traffic congestion. Over the course of the season we organised a range of activities, including various concerts and workshops for children. We also invited singers to perform

AVERAGE ATTENDANCE AT FC BARCELONA MATCHES AT THE CAMP NOU

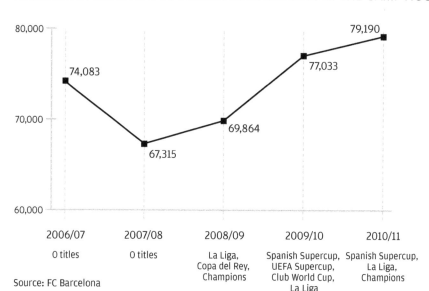

	2006/07	2007/08	2008/09	2009/10	2010/11
	0 titles	0 titles	La Liga, Copa del Rey, Champions	Spanish Supercup, UEFA Supercup, Club World Cup, La Liga	Spanish Supercup, La Liga, Champions

Source: FC Barcelona

their own version of the club anthem and perform it live in the stadium just before the team came out onto the pitch, and even hired some cheerleaders. Unfortunately, the results were not very encouraging here either. The vast majority of fans continued to arrive at the Camp Nou just in time for kick-off and the matches with the biggest crowds were those that were most interesting from a strictly sporting point of view.

It is clear, then, that – besides your margin for manoeuvre when trying to influence the date and time of fixtures (which, as we have seen, is pretty limited) – the sports marketer's ability to improve match content is, frankly, nothing more than a token effort. The appeal of a match is mostly down to the sporting element, so it is more worthwhile concentrating one's efforts on other tasks.

Your place or mine? The case of Juventus

In September 2011, Juventus opened their brand new stadium, the Juventus Stadium, and became the first club in the Italian Serie A to own their own ground and have exclusive use of it. Having played at the Stadio delle Alpi stadium since 1990 (with a brief interval at the Stadio Olimpico while construction was under way), Juventus was moving to its new home, with 42 per cent less capacity. The directors had taken the decision that their matches should be played in a smaller stadium that cut the capacity from nearly 70,000 in the Stadio delle Alpi to around 41,000 in the Juventus Stadium.

The strange thing is that, despite being Italy's most popular club, with more than five million supporters (30 per cent more than AC Milan for instance), Juventus has real problems attracting fans to its games, and it only holds sixth position in the country's spectator ranking. So the decision to reduce capacity made a lot of sense.

Although the Stadio delle Alpi was not in the least bit obsolete (it had been built in 1990 for the World Cup in Italy) it had two big disadvantages. First, it had too much capacity for the average number of spectators (around 22,000) so the atmosphere at matches was somewhat cool and the empty seats resonated on the TV screen. Second, the stands were set back a long way from the pitch, which was surrounded by an athletics track, so the fans did not have a great view and their chants of encouragement could barely be heard by the players.

With a new ground designed solely for football (with no athletics track), owned by the club, for the exclusive use of the club and much more comfortable for the spectators, Juventus achieved some spectacular results. Average attendance in the first round of the inaugural season increased by more than 50 per cent to surpass 33,000 spectators a match; the number of season ticket holders went from 14,000 to 24,000 and the football results of the first home matches were also significantly better.

COMPARISON OF JUVENTUS FC'S GROUNDS

	Stadio delle Alpi	Juventus Stadium
Capacity	70,000	41,000
Built	1990	2011
Owned by	Turin city council*	Juventus FC
Used by	Juventus FC Torino FC	Juventus FC
Sports	Football Athletics	Football
Advantages		✓ Contributes to brand because of exclusive use ✓ Better images on TV ✓ More satisfied supporters ✓ Players more motivated to win ✓ Multiplier effect

* later bought by the club to build the Juventus Stadium on the same site

The excessive stadium capacity that helped to drive the change at Juventus is not an isolated case. It is getting harder and harder to fill stadia, as a consequence of situations such as:

▸ Competition from TV broadcasts, which is provoking a change of consumer behaviour. The availability of free-to-view matches, the affordability of pay-TV rates and the arrival of new technology such as high definition and 3D TV provide more incentive to stay on the sofa or watch matches in pubs and other venues (where, incidentally, there has been a proliferation of TV screens) instead of going to the ground.
▸ The outdated nature of many grounds, meaning that many spectators find them uncomfortable.
▸ Errors in stadium design, especially when stadia are used for more than one sport. In the 1980s and 1990s it was very common to include an athletics tracks around the pitch in newly built stadia which, in practice, were used on very few occasions.
▸ The excessive number of matches played, which reduces the value of each of them. There are many fixtures whose result has very little impact on the points table.
▸ Opting for too much capacity when building stadia, as mentioned above.

Although this is a management decision, the sports marketer should have a strong opinion regarding the stadium capacity and the way it will be used (the second block in the diagram), both because of its overall impact and because of the difficulty of rectifying any mistakes that have been made. The three most common models of stadium use are:

❶ **Stadium owned by the sports property,** as a consequence of building a new venue or buying an existing one. We have already seen that this is the ideal model for a sports property that plays a lot of matches during the course of the season (particularly football clubs), although it will all depend on the availability of capital needed to make this major investment.

❷ **Strategic rental** of a stadium that is owned by a third party (generally local authorities) under a medium- to long-term contract. This is an alternative to ownership of the ground and it is very widespread in Europe because of the financial limitations of most teams, especially in the lower leagues. When the owner is a local authority, the rent tends to be subsidised (or may even be only a token rate), but the main disadvantage lies in the fact that one is very probably going to have to share the stadium with other sports properties. This is far more common in mainland Europe than in

THE BEST AND THE WORST IN EUROPE, IN TERMS OF PERCENTAGE OF
THEIR STADIUM THAT IS FILLED

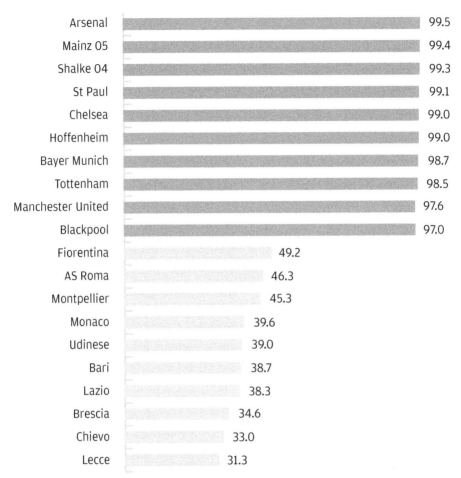

Arsenal	99.5
Mainz 05	99.4
Shalke 04	99.3
St Paul	99.1
Chelsea	99.0
Hoffenheim	99.0
Bayer Munich	98.7
Tottenham	98.5
Manchester United	97.6
Blackpool	97.0
Fiorentina	49.2
AS Roma	46.3
Montpellier	45.3
Monaco	39.6
Udinese	39.0
Bari	38.7
Lazio	38.3
Brescia	34.6
Chievo	33.0
Lecce	31.3

Source: ESPN. Domestic league matches 2010/11

the UK, although some lower-division sides will share their grounds with
other sports, such as rugby teams.

❸ **Circumstantial rental.** This model is used for one-off matches such as
tournament finals. It is also a good resource when a small team may,
on a rare occasion, have to play a much larger, even world-renowned
rival, either as a result of the way teams are paired in the draws for
tournaments with elimination rounds or because it is a friendly.

The opportunity for a sports marketer to be involved in the decision-making on the construction of a new stadium presents itself very rarely, so when it does, it becomes a huge challenge. In my case, at FC Barcelona I was able to form part of the team that outlined the main features of a potential new Camp Nou, as the original stadium was turning 50 years old in 2007. Although the project never came to fruition, for financial and political reasons, the work we did during those months was truly enjoyable and very different from our usual tasks.

The sports marketer's tasks in the decision-making process for building a new stadium

1. **Studying the attendance statistics.** Review the historical data on match attendance in detail. Pay special attention to the number of sell-out matches and the special circumstances that converged in matches with big crowd numbers.
2. **Segmenting the population and type of audience.** Know the levels of purchasing power of the local population and analyse the database of sports property members.
3. **General capacity.** Suggest a total number of seats, bearing in mind that the objective is to get the stadium filled regularly (and not just for big matches).
4. **Capacity by type of seating.** Calculate the number of seats intended for each price category.
5. **Boxes and VIP areas.** Specify the desired number of private boxes you would like (including the number of seats per box) and the number of VIP seats and exclusive areas that should be provisioned.
6. **Technical requirements for advertising.** Identify the spaces that are to be used for advertising and specify the format in each case.
7. **Personalisation and 'soul'.** Draw up a proposal on the branding elements (such as the club badge or logo and other distinguishing signs), which should be highly visible, so that the new stadium is clearly linked to the history and traditions of the sports property.

When it comes to the important decision on the seating capacity of the new ground, it is helpful to look at the case of Atlético Madrid, which has announced the building of a new stadium to be opened in 2015, with seating capacity for 70,000 spectators. It will be replacing the legendary Vicente Calderón stadium, which has a capacity of 54,476. Given that the average attendance at Atlético over the past four years is just above 41,000 spectators, and even on the assumption that the new stadium will help to significantly increase this figure, the decision to go for such high seating capacity may lead to a considerable fall in the average occupancy, with the potentially negative impact that a half-empty stadium may have on the club's general business potential.

ATLÉTICO MADRID'S AVERAGE ATTENDANCE AND OCCUPANCY AT THE OLD VS THE NEW STADIUM

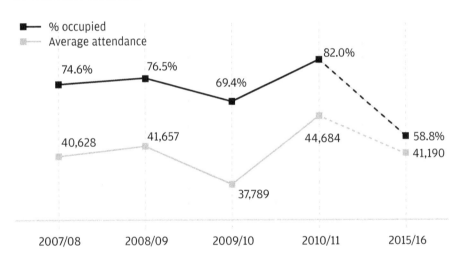

Source: ESPN

Only includes league matches

So, let's look at a summary of the sports marketer's main activities and selection criteria, when it comes to the model of stadium use:

SELECTING A MODEL OF STADIUM USE

Model of use	Sports marketer actions	Decision-making criteria
Own stadium	• Statistical analysis • Capacity proposal • Segmentation of capacity by seating categories • Technical requirements for advertising • Customisation and 'soul'	• Location and access • Investment required • Financing options • Maintenance costs
Rented stadium	• Statistical analysis • Identification of alternatives • Customisation • Artificial reduction of capacity (if more capacity than required)	• Quality of facilities • Rental costs • Location and access • Possibilities of exclusive use

Maximising attendance at each and every match has to become one of the sports marketer's obsessions, because mass attendance is, without a shadow of a doubt, the philosopher's stone that will activate every income stream of a sports property. A lot of hard work is needed to overcome one of the principal enemies of the sports marketer: the empty seat. It will be hard, well-planned work, but also very creative work.

SHOW ME THE TACTICS

❶ Draw up a scorecard of factors influencing ground attendance, customised to your sports property, and concentrate on the activities that will give you influence over the final result.

❷ Track down past stadium attendance statistics and make sure you keep them updated.

❸ Make a diagnosis of the suitability of the current stadium, based on its capacity, model of use and technical characteristics.

Goal assists

▶ If at some point you do have any decision-making power over stadium capacity, remember that it is better to have a smaller stadium that is often full than a huge stadium that only fills up once in a blue moon.

▶ Remember how important it is that the stadium looks full on television, even if it isn't. First sell the seats nearest to the pitch and then gradually move further away until you get to 'the gods'.

▶ Use some of the 'tricks of the trade' (for example, tarpaulins) to reduce ground capacity when it is clearly excessive

▶ Don't feel you should try to be involved in match content, just because non-sporting match content tends to have little influence on attendance.

▶ Keep the positioning of your sports property at the forefront of your mind in all your decision-making.

07

Hanging up the 'sold out' sign

A sold out stadium: that is what it's all about. So this chapter will be devoted to the job of 'commercialising the stadium' and will focus on the activities that a sports marketer will have to do in order to turn the spectator attendance at events into hard cash. If we go back to the diagram of commercial use of the stadium, we're now looking at the products, match day experience, and the sales and marketing phase.

THE DIAGRAM FOR COMMERCIAL EXPLOITATION OF THE STADIUM

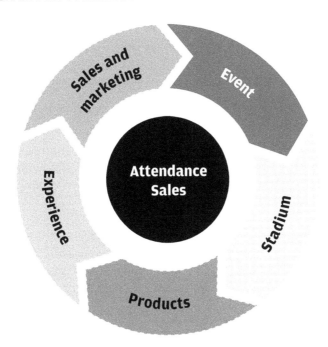

The products

The actual process of monetising stadium attendance begins after the 'stadium' block in the diagram, because it includes the main products that are to be sold in the stadium. The goal here is to translate match attendance into revenue. Remember that you need to differentiate between B2C products (those that are intended for the end consumer) and B2B products (aimed at companies), as the two groups require quite different criteria for action.

Let's look first at the more traditional products included in the commercial exploitation of the stadium: those that are aimed at the end consumers. We shall group them into three main categories:

❶ **Match tickets:** giving entry to a single match.

❷ **Season tickets:** giving entry to a set of matches, bought in advance and with a discount on the price per match compared with conventional tickets.

❸ **Consumer products** sold during match attendance, such as food, drink and official merchandise. Sports properties commonly grant the right to sell these products to a third party by way of a licensing agreement.

When it comes to the products aimed at corporate clients, we can highlight:

❶ **VIP tickets:** providing more and better content at a considerably higher price. These may include VIP season tickets.

❷ **Concessions:** allowing specialist companies to sell their consumer products in the stadium in return for a monetary fee.

❸ **Advertising:** by which companies can put up advertising messages in certain areas of the stadium. These advertising spaces can be sold individually or as part of a broader sponsorship package and they may even take the form of associating the sponsor's name with the actual stadium building or its location (naming rights).

Additionally, those sports properties that have significant silverware and a large critical mass, and that also own their stadium or have exclusive use of it, are able to commercialise the venue throughout the year, not just on match days. This can give them additional revenue through other products such as:

▸ Tours of the stadium and museum.
▸ Membership or supporter cards, within the possibilities of those sports

properties that, because of their size and success, have sold out their season tickets and still have a demand for an actual connection from supporters that are unable to attend matches with any regularity.

▶ Non-sporting events and concerts.
▶ Hire of venue facilities for corporate events such as sales conventions or advertising commercial shoots.

SALEABLE PRODUCTS IN THE STADIUM

	B2C	B2B
Match days	Tickets	VIP tickets and season tickets
	Season tickets	Concessions
	Food, drink and merchandising	Advertising
Non-match days	Membership card	Non-sporting events
	Stadium tour	Venue hire
	Museum	

Matchgoers' experience through touch points

In June 2011, I attended a speech in Barcelona given by the director of operations at Manchester United, Michael Bolingbroke. During his talk I first associated the term 'touch points' with the experience of attending a match at a stadium. As Michael explained, a spectator's experience of a match at a stadium is full of touch points between them and the sports property, and these touch points have a decisive influence on the fan's general level of satisfaction, above and beyond the actual spectacle on the pitch. The sports marketer should focus on ensuring that each and every one of these touch points is valued as highly as possible by the spectator because, taken as one, these evaluations and the final score of the match will make up the general level of satisfaction that will determine repeat visits, consumption in the stadium and the price they are willing to pay for a ticket.

I have identified ten touch points for supporters attending a match at the ground and we shall look at them all in detail below. It is worth remembering the two types of groups that we are targeting through our commercialisation plans, because they both have different expectations and require very different action strategies: conventional customers (B2C) and VIP or corporate clients (B2B).

So let's describe what might be considered an ideal day at the ground through the touch points that occur before, during and after a match.

THE TEN TOUCH POINTS BETWEEN A SPORTS PROPERTY AND A SPECTATOR

Before	During the match		After
❶ **Information** ❷ **Buying the ticket**	❸ **Access to the ground** ❹ **Entrance to the ground** ❺ **Seat**	❻ **Information** ❼ **Food** ❽ **Shops** ❾ **Toilets**	❿ *Feedback*

❶ **Information.** The process begins with the way the sports property communicates the day and time of the match, the price of tickets and the channels through which they can be bought. The information is available and highly visible on the official website and is also spread through social networking sites. There is also a customer information number that is not continuously engaged, and the advisers who answer it are friendly and have an answer to the most frequently asked questions. The telephone number for business clients is a separate and exclusive one.

❷ **Buying the ticket.** The purchasing channels function correctly, do not get overloaded and are open in hours compatible with normal working hours. Credit and debit cards are accepted by all channels. Tickets can also be bought on the internet through a fully secure payment process. If the ticket is not given out at the time of purchase, the collection method is convenient and does not entail any additional costs or queuing. Companies that wish to can request an invoice with their details on, which they will receive by email or normal post, hassle-free.

❸ **Access to the ground.** There is public transport to the stadium that is also in operation after the match has ended (in Germany, public transport for supporters is free on match days, with match tickets doubling as train passes). For those opting to come in their own vehicle, there is sufficient parking space in the area. VIP clients can hire a parking space that should not be too far from the ground.

❹ **Entrance to the ground.** There are enough entrances into the stadium and the entry control system functions correctly. One can enter the ground without pushing and shoving or overcrowding.

❺ Seat. Signage will show the location of seats and, if in doubt, there are stewards available to help. The stadium is fitted with lifts or escalators to reach the higher stands. When one reaches one's seat, it is clean and, of course, unoccupied. VIP clients have a special entrance, the seats are more comfortable than the conventional ones and there is a good view of the pitch.

❻ Information. From any seat in the stadium one can at least see the scoreboard and the playing time that has passed. VIP clients will also be given a team sheet and will have access to exclusive rooms fitted with TV screens.

❼ Food. The queue for bars and restaurants is not too long and they do not run out of stock too quickly. The food is of good quality, prices are not extortionate and one can pay with a credit or debit card. VIP clients get their food and drink free of charge in their exclusive areas or in their private box; food and drink is varied and in sufficient quantity for all the people present who, naturally, do not have to queue for it. Staff are very friendly. The number of people with access to the VIP areas matches the room capacity.

❽ Shops. Licensed products can be bought in the official shops, with at least the official home team kit being available (or both team kits at a neutral ground). All sizes are available. The queue is not too long.

❾ Toilets. The toilets are well signed and clean. There are enough of them to avoid crowding and excessive queuing.

❿ Feedback. Customers have channels through which to make complaints or suggestions and when they do, they get a response. Sports property staff should make random calls to customers to find out their views on the quality of service and get suggestions for improvement.

Lack of attention to customer satisfaction often leads to unsatisfactory experiences and this is undoubtedly one of the causes of falling crowd numbers at grounds. So, despite the impossibility of influencing factors as important as the beauty of the game that has been played or the final match result, the sports marketer should still take responsibility for optimising the spectator experience at the ground (the next block in the diagram for commercial exploitation of the stadium, after products). To do so, you should lead and carry out the following activities:

❶ **Informing** potential customers of the dates and times of matches and how to buy tickets.

❷ **Defining the content, process and services** of all the products on offer.

❸ **Assigning customer service staff,** based on the sports property's available resources. Staff should also get proper training.

❹ **Getting the equipment, facilities and technology** needed from the managers of the appropriate departments, also based on available resources.

❺ **Exercising control and vigilance** of the level of quality provided by the restaurants, official stores or ticket sales channels.

❻ **Opening lines of communication** that will let you find out customer opinion and bear these opinions in mind when taking management decisions.

In my time as a sports marketer, I have experienced different kinds of touch points. On the positive side, I remember the 2003 Super Bowl at the Qualcomm Stadium in San Diego, where we were given closed-circuit radio sets that carried commentary on the match specifically for people who hadn't mastered the rules of the game (such as me, for example). I was also pleased by how well I could see the match from the very back rows of the Allianz Arena in Munich at the France–Portugal semi-final of the 2006 World Cup. And later, I was pleasantly surprised at how, when leaving the VIP room at the UEFA Super Cup of 2011 (held in Monaco), the UEFA staff had their umbrellas at the ready to help us stay dry for the ten metres that separated the exit from the door of the coach, despite the downpour. I also recall how, at a match at Stamford Bridge in 2009, my son Esteve had a great time having pictures taken of himself in front of a backdrop that made it look like he was being photographed with the Chelsea players.

Conversely, in February 2006 I was amazed that, in a VIP room at Stamford Bridge during the last-16 round of the Champions League between Chelsea and FC Barcelona, we were charged for the drinks that we (together with the actual president of the club) had ordered. I faced the same situation in January 2013 when Queens Park Rangers were hosting Manchester City FC in a league match, and the chief financial officer of the latter, Jorge Chumillas, and myself had to pay cash (not even credit cards were accepted) for a couple of beers in a VIP room at Loftus Road. On the various occasions that I have been able to attend matches at Old Trafford, I have always been struck by the fact that there were no big screens showing live video.

STAMFORD BRIDGE, 2009

When it comes to my time at FC Barcelona, I have no hesitation in recognising that I did not pay enough attention to managing customer satisfaction. We believed that customer satisfaction depended basically on the team's style of play and on the match result, and we mostly focused on solving the issues that, because of repeated complaints, had become significant.

It is true that resources are limited and it is not possible to have everything under control, but the sports marketer should still come up with a list of priorities for managing the spectator experience and touch points, because they will have an impact on revenue potential further down the line.

The six Ps marketing mix

Now we come to the fifth and final element, where the sports marketer converts attendance into cash – this includes all the actual sales and marketing activities.

At the ESADE Business School in Barcelona, where I was fortunate enough to study, the first thing they taught us about marketing was the four Ps: product, price, promotion and place, which are key to a marketing manager's ability to influence his company's results.

When we're looking at sports marketing and stadium exploitation I use, we shall use the four Ps as a starting point, and, with apologies to purists, I add a further two Ps. So we have a marketing mix made up of six elements: people (segmentation); product; price; place (distribution channels); publicity (communication); and promotion.

❶ **People (segmentation).** The first job in the marketing mix involves deciding beforehand on the buyer profile that best fits each of the products related to ground attendance. The idea is to identify different groups of customers that, based on various segmentation variables, will then lead to specific action plans for each group. As you can see in the table below, by using three variables (place of residence, degree of emotional engagement with the sports property and the customer's purchasing power) we can start to identify six groups of buyers of different ticket categories.

SIMPLIFIED SEGMENTATION OF TICKET BUYERS

Buyer categories	Fanatics	Casual buyers	Companies
Same town or region*	Season tickets VIP tickets	Tickets	VIP season tickets
The rest	Tickets VIP tickets	Tickets	VIP tickets

* Defined as the buyer can drive to the ground in less than two hours

❷ **Product.** In April 2011, I paid the not inconsiderable sum of €250 per ticket to invite some clients of my company Prime Time Sport to the final of the Copa del Rey between Real Madrid and FC Barcelona in Valencia. I was absolutely astonished by the terrible design of the ticket itself and the flimsy paper on which it was printed. Even though the most important thing was, of course, the spectacular event to which this ticket gave access, this example does serve to remind us that the sports marketer, as well as working to carefully define the services and content associated with a ticket or a season ticket (as I mentioned when describing the touch points), is also responsible for the more tangible aspects of the products (such as the paper used for tickets or plastic used for season tickets) and for ensuring that they are functional.

❸ **Price.** Price is not a defining factor when it comes to selling tickets. I know that this may come across as a pretty controversial statement and that many readers will disagree. I shall explain myself by referring to a couple of real situations. On 10 November 2009, with a very cold spell forecast, FC Barcelona was at home to play the return match in the last 32 of the Copa del Rey against Cultural Leonesa (2nd division B), and it was decided to set the ticket prices very low indeed, starting at around €5. The tie had already been pretty much decided in the first match as Barça won 0-2 in Leon and the match was also being broadcast live on open-access TV at 10 p.m. Despite the affordable prices, only 26,322 spectators came to the Camp Nou. Whether we had given free entry or tickets at twice the price (say, €10 each), the level of attendance would have been more or less the same.

At the other end of the scale, UEFA was severely criticised in the media for fixing prices of £150–£300 for tickets to the Champions League final played at Wembley Stadium on 28 May 2011 between FC Barcelona and Manchester United. Because this was an event of exceptionally high public interest, and despite the exorbitant price of the tickets, UEFA quickly sold all available tickets and 87,695 spectators packed out the stadium. UEFA could have priced the tickets even higher, and the event would still have been a sell-out.

These two extreme examples serve to remind us that, as we saw at the beginning of this chapter, high attendance levels are normally linked to strictly sporting factors, and the sports marketer's ability to exert any influence on them (including through ticket prices) is pretty limited. Nevertheless, I make the following recommendations when it comes to deciding on ticket prices:

▶ Set the prices as high as possible for matches of exceptional interest, to the limit accepted by public opinion (should you choose to take it into account).

▶ Do not set derisory prices for matches classed as 'unsellable' because it is yet to be proven that this will attract more people. It also detracts from the event's value and sacrifices profitability unnecessarily.

▶ Have an early bird discount, particularly when the day and time of the match is not yet known at the time of purchase.

▶ Reward the purchase of tickets for several matches at a time, especially for every match of the season.

▶ Avoid resorting to last-minute discounts on a regular basis, as this will encourage buyers to hold out for these to kick in, and will put an end to early purchasing.

❹ **Place (distribution channels).** As with conventional marketing, your success in commercialising the stadium will largely depend on how well you develop the right distribution strategy. Both when using your own ticket sales channels (mainly ticket booths at the ground and on for the website) and third party channels, a sports property's distribution channels should at the very least meet the following requirements:

▶ Have as many points of sale as possible, both physical and online.

▶ Have at least one option (usually the website) that is operational 24/7, 365 days of the year and accessible from every corner of the globe.

▶ Set up a mechanism that lets the public identify which points of sale are official.

▶ And, of course, both the sport property itself and any third party channels must offer the best possible purchasing experience at every sale (remember the touch points).

Coach's notebook

Tickets for sports events should be available at as many places as possible, at all times, and through purchasing and collection processes that work correctly and are easy to use.

I remember that one of my little disappointments as chief commercial and marketing officer at FC Barcelona was that I was not able to break into the exclusive rights for ticket sales held by the Catalan bank, La Caixa (more specifically, its ServiCaixa system, today owned by Ticketmaster) in the negotiations to broaden the sponsorship contract. Despite the fact that it was a system that worked well (and with distribution points all over Spain), I wanted to increase the points of sale for tickets even further, and we had proposals from the department store El Corte Inglés and the media and culture chain Fnac, for example. When negotiating the new sponsorship contract in 2003, I tried every which way I could to get La Caixa to agree to give up the exclusivity of ServiCaixa, but it was completely impossible because at that point the bank considered it an absolutely crucial part of the new agreement. Today, and as a result of agreements negotiated after my departure from the club, ServiCaixa no longer has the exclusive rights to sell FC Barcelona tickets, which are now available to buy through other channels.

❺ Publicity (communication). In November 2011, the sports marketers at Real Madrid faced an unusual challenge. Their match at the Santiago Bernabéu against Osasuna, of Pamplona, had been scheduled for

Sunday 6 November at 12 noon. In order to maximise TV viewing figures in Asia, for the first time in history, the club was to play a league match at home before lunchtime. Little could the ticket-sellers imagine that it was precisely the novelty of the timing that was to become their best ally. As soon as the LFP (Liga de Fútbol Profesional) confirmed the news, the media did not stop generating content regarding the time of the match. Journalists wrote about the change to the training times, the planning of mealtimes and the possibility of taking the kids along (as kick-off in Spain is usually in the evening, making it less family-friendly). The club directors also helped by making public statements in support of the unusual time. Indeed, the 'aperitif match' got the best promotion money could buy without actually having to spend a single euro on advertising. And the result could hardly have been better: a stadium packed to the rafters with 83,000 spectators and a shower of home goals (7-1) on the pitch. History repeated itself in February 2013, when FC Barcelona hosted Getafe at the Camp Nou, also at 12 noon (the first Barça match at that hour for 47 years). Barça's stadium was filled with 85,610 people, one of the best attendance records of the season.

Editorial coverage of match-related news is, of course, the most natural and the cheapest way of promoting ticket sales, so the sports marketer should constantly work to generate and distribute match news or, depending on the level of interest, simply make the media's job easier (for example, by giving them access to training sessions). Editorial coverage is, then, one of the four main communication and advertising activities when it comes to ticket sales:

Ⓐ Free editorial coverage.

Ⓑ Advertising on own media (website, club spaces on social networks, etc.).

Ⓒ Conventional paid advertising or in the form of an exchange. As we shall see later, on certain occasions, news coverage is insufficient or will not refer to all the content that you want to communicate, so it will be necessary to resort to buying specific spaces. This can also be very useful for advertising VIP products aimed at companies, to promote advance ticket purchasing for future matches.

Ⓓ Direct communication to the databases we have available.

❻ Promotion. I am not a big fan of organising promotions that centre on gifts or discounts for selling tickets, as I don't think that this is a proven method of increasing sales. If used too often it also detracts value from the matches and makes it harder to then go back to normal pricing. For example, in my early days at FC Barcelona, I was horrified to discover that around 3,000 tickets were given away for every match, which had created a culture among supporters in the city of trying to get a free ticket before they even thought of buying one.

However, there are some promotional drives that can be successful in certain circumstances, such as:

▸ Gifts or benefits when buying season tickets, such as financing schemes to help spread the cost.

▸ Mini-season tickets for several matches, capitalising on the fact that some of them have exceptional commercial appeal.

▸ Special promotions for companies that buy VIP products. For example, at FC Barcelona one thing that worked very well for us was giving away the last matches of the season in progress to companies that bought VIP packages for the following season.

Ticket sales scenarios

In late 2002, as a representative of FC Barcelona, I attended a course organised by Euroleague Basketball and given by the consultant Jon Spoelstra. The purpose of the course was to give new ideas to teams taking part in a tournament on how to sell events. The consultant, a consummate expert in ticket sales, having worked for various teams in the NBA, kept repeating that the most important thing for a ticket sales manager to do was to develop the 'sold out mentality'. According to this theory, as soon as he or she knows the fixtures calendar for the season, the sports marketer should select a number of games (from four to six) that *a priori* have the potential to sell out, concentrating his selling efforts into getting the tickets for these matches sold out as soon as possible. That way, news of each sold out match will send a message to potential buyers that there is a risk they won't get tickets and this will create a demand for the rest of the matches that are, in theory, less appealing. It is only once the 'sold out' target has been met that the sports marketer should put more work into the other fixtures. Jon Spoelstra's theory was rounded off with another very thought-provoking message: 'Do not spend a single minute on unsellable matches or on matches of exceptional interest; the former will not sell well, whatever you do, and the latter will sell themselves without you having to do anything.'

When I heard those words, I was just taking my first steps as a sports marketer, and the lessons I learned on that course shaped the way I saw the job of commercialising the stadium and selling tickets. So much so that straight after finishing the course I decided to instil the 'sold out mentality' in our ticket sales team at FC Barcelona. But Francesc Lladós, who was responsible for the ticket office at the time, warned me of the difficulty of selling tickets with this new philosophy, given that in the Spanish La Liga, match schedules were only made public ten days in advance.

He had a fair point. Having a fixtures calendar for the season in advance (as a result of the draw), along with the exact kick-off times of all matches (nowadays as a result of TV scheduling requirements) is absolutely essential for being able to apply these different professional strategies of ticket sales.

So, when putting these strategies into practice and facing up to the challenge of bringing in as much money as possible through single and season ticket sales, I have identified six scenarios, each of them requiring a different marketing mix from the sports marketer: (1) advance sales; (2) the unsellable match; (3) the match of exceptional interest; (4) season ticket sales; (5) ownership of season tickets; and (6) VIP ticket sales.

❶ **Advance sales scenario.** Every year in the middle of June before the start of the competition, the English Premier League holds a draw to determine the fixtures list. This league is the earliest to fix their schedule in Europe and sports marketers are eternally grateful for it, as they get the fixture dates two months in advance. While the exact match times are not yet known, with the fixtures list in one's hand you can start advance sales of match tickets. This scenario, similar to what occurs in the sale of airline seats, is based on the goal of selling as many tickets beforehand as possible, favouring the more 'organised' buyers and penalising the stragglers. Let's look at the most important elements of this type of selling and how the six Ps marketing mix is used in this scenario:

  ▶ *Segmentation (people):* essentially aiming at casual buyers, fans who live away or fans of the rival team.
  ▶ *Price/promotion:* establishing a base tariff and applying discounts based on how far in advance the purchase is made. Maximising discounts (50 per cent or more) for purchases made more than five or six months ahead, without precise knowledge of match times.
  ▶ *Distribution channels (place):* open at their usual times and functioning correctly.
  ▶ *Communication (publicity):* using the club's own media, buying conventional advertising space, notifying databases.
  ▶ *Sales mentality (product):* proactive.

❷ **The unsellable match.** Unfortunately for the sports marketer, the fixture list for the season inevitably means that there are matches where, whatever you do, attendance will be very low. In these cases, the message is clear: do not waste a single minute on promoting unsellable events and put your effort into selling other matches where you have a better chance of commercial success.

The unsellable match

❶ The rival team is a very lowly one.

❷ The result of the match determines nothing.

❸ The team is not having a good season.

❹ The coaches are unlikely to bring out their best players.

❺ The date and time of the match have been announced shortly beforehand.

❻ The match is played mid-week on a working day.

❼ The match is being broadcast on open-access TV.

❽ The weather forecast is bad (cold and/or rain).

❾ There is a home match scheduled for the weekend before or after.

❿ A popular TV programme is on at the same time.

❸ The match of exceptional interest. Now and again, some sports marketers get the chance to work on events that are so special that they simply 'sell themselves'. The final of a major tournament, an FC Barcelona–Real Madrid *clásico*, a match that will decide whether the team will remain in the division or a derby between two big rivals are examples of sports events of exceptional interest, where the sports marketer's only job is to set the price at the upper limit permitted by public opinion. Just as with unsellable matches, any other effort should be put into selling other matches.

❹ Season ticket sales. Despite having at least two pages a day of news coverage, AC Milan and Inter traditionally insert conventional advertising for season tickets in *La Gazzetta dello Sport*. Given that information on season tickets does not form part of the content that journalists are interested in covering and also the need to communicate details such as prices and different seating areas, you need to buy advertising space that will give you complete control over the content. Attracting the maximum number of season ticket sales possible at the start of the season is of strategic importance to most sports properties because it is a guarantee of revenue, a significant injection of cash and a reduction in the number of seats that have to be sold as single tickets.

Attracting buyers of season tickets requires the sports marketer's full attention, a proactive sales mentality and intensive use of every element in the marketing mix:

▶ *Segmentation (People)*: aimed at fans that live in the same town or region.

- *Product:* specifying the number of matches and the tournaments included and the location of the seat.
- *Price:* the average cost per match should be at least 20 per cent lower than if one bought separate tickets for each match.
- *Distribution channels (Place):* as well as the usual ones, specific channels are required, especially with lines to sales advisers, due to the large amount of information that has to be given.
- *Communication (Publicity):* through the sports property's own media, conventional advertising campaigns and information sent to the people on your databases. Bear in mind that the especially creative campaigns can bring the added bonus of free media coverage.
- *Promotion:* exclusive windows of opportunity for season ticket holders to choose their seat, financing schemes to spread the cost, exclusive gifts related to the sports property, and so on.

ADVERTISING FOR SEASON TICKETS TO INTER MILAN 2011/12

⑤ **Ownership of season tickets.** This scenario only occurs when the demand for season tickets is significantly higher than ground capacity, year after year. This is the case for major teams such as Real Madrid, FC Barcelona and Manchester United, and a good number of German teams, such as Bayern Munich, Mainz 05 and Schalke 04. It is almost as though the season ticket holders were the actual owners of the seat because they have had them for years and, in some cases, they have been in the family for several generations, and they have preference when it comes to reserving them. In this scenario, the work of the sports marketer focuses on selling the few tickets that are still available for each match and, fundamentally, it is limited to:

► *Product:* set an upper limit on season tickets so that there are tickets available for each match, to be sold at a higher price or to comply with regulations that require one to reserve a number of seats for supporters of the rival team (5 per cent of total capacity in the case of the UEFA Champions League).

► *Communication (Publicity):* if demand usually outstrips supply, then supporters will assume that it will be impossible to get their hands on a ticket, so it will occasionally be necessary to notify them (through the press, your own media or advertising campaigns) that there are still tickets available. For example, in the 2011/12 season, FC Barcelona launched an ad campaign to sell La Liga match tickets. In it, the phrase 'tickets still available' was highlighted.

SUMMARY OF THE MARKETING MIX FOR EACH TICKET SALES SCENARIO

Marketing mix	Advance sales	Unsellable match	Exceptional match	Season tickets
Segmentation	Not hardcore local fans Casual fans	—	—	Local fans
Product	Single tickets	Single tickets	Single tickets	
Price	Basic	Basic	Very high	Low
Distribution channels	Open and working	Open and working	Open and working	Add phone and face-to-face
Communication	Own media Advertising Database	News coverage	News coverage	Own media Advertising Database
Promotion	'Early bird' discounts	—	—	Gifts Other benefits
Sales mentality	Proactive	Reactive	Reactive	Proactive

6 **VIP ticket sales.** The higher profits made by products sold to companies, in the form of VIP match tickets or season tickets (which, in the world of sports marketing, is known as 'hospitality') and the unique nature of this group of potential buyers translates into a need to create a maximum intensity and completely different marketing mix.

▸ *Segmentation (People):* products that fundamentally target companies.

▸ *Product:* more exclusive touch points, contents and services.

▸ *Price:* the price per match of a VIP ticket is at least four times that of the most expensive standard ticket.

▸ *Distribution channels (Place):* specific sales and distribution channels are required.

▸ *Communication (Publicity):* own media, conventional advertising in specialist magazines targeting companies, and use of databases.

▸ *Promotion:* player-signed kit, extra matches included, based on the duration of the season ticket that has been purchased, the chance to meet players and directors in person, and so on.

ADVERTISING FOR THE VIP SCHEME AT AC MILAN 2011/12

Concessions, advertising and other products

So, tickets for matches are just one of the products the sports marketer should focus on. Of all the others that exist, let's focus on concessions to third parties (mainly related to consumption at the stadium), advertising sales and naming rights. In the table below are some recommendations on how to sell these three product categories.

SELLING CONCESSIONS, ADVERTISING AND NAMING RIGHTS

Products	Considerations	Key success factors
Concessions	• Criteria for selecting licensees: experience, investments, financial capacity and quality of products • e.g. cafes, restaurants, official stores, betting shops	• Level of attendance • Right choice of licensee • Management of the touch points
Advertising	• Possibility of one-off purchase or as part of broader sponsorship package • e.g. hoardings, scoreboards	• Sporting success • Level of attendance • TV coverage
Naming rights	• Commercial brand gives its name to a stadium or a tournament • Important to bear in mind how it fits with brands in sponsorship programme	• New stadia • Media are on board with using the new name

There are, of course, many other products that can be sold at a sport event, such as the match programme and photographs of the kids with the team, as well as food, drink and merchandise should one choose to sell these oneself (as opposed to granting the rights to third parties). As such the sports marketer's entrepreneurial mindset will be very welcome here, although the products will have to meet the following requirements:

▶ The products must be profitable (the price must be higher than the cost) and not require major investment.
▶ They should have a positive impact on the match day experience (touch points).
▶ They should not add another level of complexity to your management tasks.

The sales action plan

We shall end this chapter by once again insisting on the importance of developing and sharing with the sports property organisation documents that contain, in black and white, the actions plans that we aim to implement. We should therefore draw up a ticket sales action plan that should at least include the following:

▶ **An inventory of available tickets,** taking into account the total number of matches planned and the number assigned to each category (ticket price layering, single versus season tickets, standard versus VIP tickets).

▶ **Analysis of the fixtures list** (or the decisions on fixtures, if one has any say in that), initially grouped into three sets: sold out target; unsellable; and exceptional interest.

▶ **Ticket sales targets,** both in terms of number and of revenue, for each of the categories and for every match.

▶ **Calendar of sales and marketing activities,** specifying an implementation timeline for each of them.

▶ **Costing budget** for developing the proposed plan and hitting the sales targets.

Here comes the money! And this is just the start. Let's now go back to our roadmap, for the next revenue opportunity.

THE SPORTS MARKETER'S ACTIVITIES AROUND COMMERCIAL EXPLOITATION OF THE STADIUM

SHOW ME THE TACTICS

❶ Decide and define the products to be sold at the ground, specifying which of them will be sold through concessions.

❷ Identify the touch points in the match attendance experience and make an assessment of the level of quality that is being provided.

❸ Set up communication channels to receive and take into account spectator feedback.

❹ Develop the six Ps marketing mix for every ticket sales scenario.

❺ Include all the information in the sales action plan, distribute it to the relevant people and update it regularly to show whether you are hitting targets.

Goal assists

▸ Replicate the match attendance experience: do it yourself, anonymously, as though you were just another spectator.

▸ Remember how important it is that season ticket holders, even if they have already paid for their ticket, actually come to the stadium.

▸ When opening up the channels of communication to get feedback from spectators, remember that it is important to always give a response and to take the suggestions into account.

▸ Concentrate your investment into conventional advertising when encouraging supporters to buy tickets for future matches in advance, in order to attract new season ticket holders and sell VIP products, but not to promote forthcoming matches that will get enough editorial coverage on their own.

▸ Think good and hard before lowering ticket prices to increase match attendance. If the match is unsellable, all this will do is decrease profitability.

▸ Analyse in great detail the data you have before you decide to class a match as being 'of exceptional interest'. Bear in mind that if you set ticket prices very high and the match is not of exceptional appeal, the only thing you'll do is create an empty stadium.

▸ Think twice before giving away match tickets, even if you know the stadium is not going to fill.

▸ Split the season into chunks so that you can set yourself sell-out targets over shorter time frames (for example, three months).

- ▶ Have a big celebration with your team whenever you get a sell-out match and try to get it mentioned in the media.
- ▶ Keep the positioning of your sports property at the forefront of your mind in all your decision-making.

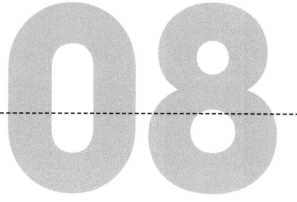

Sponsorship rights or bust

'We can sort this out with a couple more sponsors'; 'we'll ask the sponsors for more cash and it'll all be sorted'. These are phrases that are often heard in the meeting rooms and corridors of sports properties offices. Faced with the constant need to increase revenue, sponsorship generally comes up as the most attractive and profitable product, because it has almost no associated costs. But capturing sponsors is not as easy as that, in this day and age, and neither is there unlimited potential for growth.

Attracting sponsors is, in effect, one of the sports marketer's principal obsessions and occupations and the next few stages on our route to where the money is will be devoted to this topic. As well as now and again winning new sponsorship contracts, our objective is to identify long-term travelling companions who, through financial contributions and advertising campaigns based on our legally held rights, help to achieve sustained revenue growth and to promote our sports property in general. When it comes down to it, we not only want sponsors: we want partners.

But before we really delve into the process of attracting advertisers and sponsors, we need to find our way around the complex network of rights and advertising spaces – crucial if you want to get as much 'performance' as possible (cash, obviously) from all the commercial options that are available.

A tough terrain

The process of identifying advertisers and new sponsors takes place in a landscape that is full of challenges and obstacles that the sports marketer must face with hard work, good organisational skills, creativity and an entrepreneurial spirit. Some of these challenges are:

▶ Cuts to companies' marketing and advertising budgets against the general backdrop of economic austerity, particularly in Europe.

▶ The polarisation that is creating an ever-widening gap between a small, elite group of sports properties and all the rest. The former – such as FIFA, UEFA and the big global clubs – manage to increase their revenue year on year and have more sponsorship requests than they can cater for. The others (the vast majority) have an ever tougher job not just to attract but even to retain sponsors.

▶ Growing and varied competition from other sponsorship options and from conventional advertising means that proposals start to pile up on the desks of marketing directors in companies with money to invest.

▶ Overlap of rights caused by the possibility that apparently similar rights can form part of different sponsorship programmes. So, for example, in certain circumstances three different companies can have rights to the same player by sponsoring his club, his national squad or reaching an agreement for the right of use of his personal image.

POLARISATION OF SPONSORSHIP REVENUE

League	Teams	Sponsorship revenue of select teams as % of total across league
La Liga	Real Madrid FC Barcelona	69%
Premier League	Manchester United Liverpool Manchester City Chelsea	61%
Serie A	AC Milan Inter Milan Juventus Napoli	58%

Source: Annual Review of Football Finance, Deloitte
Data for the 2011/12 season

The winning three-leaf clover

My first steps in the world of sponsorship were about as traumatic as it comes. When I joined FC Barcelona and asked for copies of the club's various sponsorship contracts, I got several unpleasant surprises. As well as a few conventional sponsorship contracts, there were others through which the club had granted use of certain assets and advertising spaces to various specialist companies. For example, the advertising hoardings at the stadium had been sold to Santa Monica Sports, the advertising space on the scoreboard to ISO and the stadium canopies to Advertis. Meanwhile, Grupo Godó and ADI were in charge of producing the official club magazine and IMG produced the website (as we saw in Chapter 4), in return for exclusive rights to sell their advertising space. And as if that was not enough, my arrival coincided with an exclusive transfer of all sponsorship rights for several years, in return for a considerable sum of money to the company Havas Sports, which then held the responsibility for finding new sponsors.

As a consequence of this transfer of key rights and advertising spaces as stipulated in these contracts, there were at least six different companies on the market legitimately selling FC Barcelona-related commercial assets (not including any attempts we at the club might be making). In other words, a single potential client could be contacted by six different sales representatives offering different types of links with the club. Bearing in mind that all these companies were working without any form of coordination between them, the perceived value was negatively impacted by this situation and the danger was that several brands within the same industry could have bought one of the products. It was a completely unfeasible way to win strategic sponsorship contracts for the club.

As I found myself in this nightmarish situation, more than once I asked myself what I actually had the power to do in this role. So, from the word go, I made the decision to regain control of each and every right that had been transferred, however long it took.

The commercial use of a sports property's assets is based on the successful management of three fundamental concepts:

❶ **The significance of the commercial product.** The result of combining the positioning, brands, media exposure and level of critical mass that were analysed in detail in Parts I and II of this book. If you have positioned your sport property to be something people want to be a part of, this will be much easier.

❷ **The availability of rights.** Do you have ownership or control of all or most of the following rights?
  ▶ The right to place advertising at the sports property events and activities.
  ▶ The right to get the actual, visible involvement of players and coaches and image rights to the use of the content that this generates.
  ▶ The right to use images and the distinguishing elements of the club.

❸ **Well-managed advertising spaces.** Identification, management and maintenance of the advertising spaces and media that we sell and for which we will try to attract as much press exposure as possible during the various events and activities.

Coach's notebook

A sports property's capacity to consolidate sponsorship revenue in the medium to long term is directly proportional to the level of availability and control it has vis-à-vis the right to place advertising, use players and use the images and distinguishing elements.

Together, the three concepts act as the starting point for our advertising and sponsorship work.

If fortune, in the shape of sporting success, is also on our side, we can then add the fourth concept to make a 'lucky clover'. Indeed, titles and sporting success are a massive boost for increasing commercial and sponsorship revenue (and sporting failure has the opposite effect). Nevertheless, and given the sports marketer's lack of real influence on sporting results, in our search for the money it will be difficult to speculate on the basis of sporting success. So we just have to assume that we will achieve successful sponsorship management by using our winning (one leaf short) three-leafed clover.

THE WINNING THREE-LEAF CLOVER

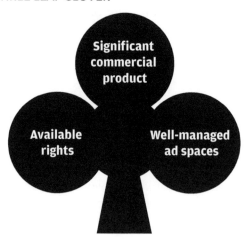

Solving the sudoku of commercial rights

- ▶ A Spanish beer company, Mahou, hired David Villa – a player for FC Barcelona and the Spanish national side – as its ambassador. As part of this contract, Mahou earned the right to shoot various TV commercials using Villa's personal image rights (in normal clothing).
- ▶ The Damm beer company, as a sponsor of FC Barcelona, has the right to use the official image rights (wearing club kit) of the entire squad, including David Villa, in its advertising.
- ▶ Cruzcampo, the official beer of the national side, can use the image of the team's players wearing the official kit of the Spanish national team, which also includes David Villa.
- ▶ Heineken, as official sponsor of the UEFA Champions League, has the right to reproduce match images, which may include FC Barcelona and David Villa, in its communications.
- ▶ Budweiser sponsors the World Cup in which the Spanish national team (and, of course, David Villa) play.

So five brands that compete against each other for a share of the beer market can all be more or less directly associated with the footballer David Villa, through five different sponsorship schemes with different sports properties. This creates a complex web of rights that the sports marketer has to learn to navigate with ease, if he wants to sell sponsorship of his sports property with any guarantee of success.

To begin solving your very own sudoku, you first have to analyse what rights you have when it comes to the different events and activities in which your sports property takes part.

Let's group them into three main categories:

❶ **Sports activity.** Matches, training sessions, official tournament press conferences and photo calls. The most common types of rights ownership are:
  - ▶ **Domestic competition:** rights to advertising at matches fall to the home team. Depending on the contracts that have been signed, tournament organisers can buy or use space (or even insist on inserting it) for their own sponsors.
  - ▶ **Finals and special tournaments:** the sports property organising the tournament (for example, UEFA) holds all the rights to advertising in the stadium, except for any advertising found on the teams' kits. This may also include giving exclusive press conferences. The transfer of these rights allows teams to take part in the competition and gives access to monetary payments, normally linked to sporting results.

- **Training sessions and team gatherings**: advertising at the club training facilities and on players' kits is controlled by the club.
- **Players' participation and image rights.** These are owned by the club for which they play, which usually acquires them as one of the terms and conditions in the player's employment contracts.

❷ **Communication activity.** Anything organised by the sports property to achieve free coverage in the media, such as press conferences, exclusive interviews or media events of any kind. Ownership of advertising and players' participation and image rights usually falls to the sports property organising the event.

❸ **Advertising.** Shoots for TV commercials, photography sessions and functions organised by the companies that are advertising, with the participation of players and/or technical staff, to then be disseminated for the purposes of advertising. This can involve the use of four different types of rights:

- **Official players' rights:** when the player is filmed or photographed wearing the official team kit.
- **Personal players' rights:** dressed in normal clothing (without showing the distinguishing symbols of any sports property).
- **Archive images** of matches or training sessions to be used in sponsors' advertising campaigns. They often have to be bought back from the TV stations that acquired the rights in the past.
- **Distinguishing symbols** of the sports property, such as the club badge, the official team kit or the trophy.

EXAMPLES OF ADVERTISING

1

2

3

4

5

6

7

8

9

EXAMPLES OF THE USE OF RIGHTS FOR ADVERTISING CAMPAIGNS

Advertiser	No.	Sports properties			
		Distinguishing symbols	Official player's rights		Personal player's rights
			Group	Individual	
Nivea	1	England squad			
Nike	2	Portugal squad		C. Ronaldo	Piqué
Konami	3	Real Madrid Champions League Europa League		C. Ronaldo	
EA Sports	4	Manchester United		Rooney	
Braun	5				Mourinho
Adidas	6	AC Milan	Cassano Ibrahimovic Pato Van Bommel Seedorf Robinho		
Seiko	7	FC Barcelona	Messi Alexis Iniesta Thiago Fábregas		
Adidas	8	Argentina squad		Messi	
Continental	9	Brazil 2014 Spain squad	Llorente Torres Casillas Iniesta Piqué		

In the above examples of press advertisements, you can clearly see the different ways in which commercial brands use rights and trademarks. Nike and Konami ads use Cristiano Ronaldo's rights as a player for the Portuguese national side and for Real Madrid, respectively. Braun has used its contract to use the personal image rights of José Mourinho (who appears dressed in normal clothing). Nivea publicises its sponsorship of the English national squad by claiming that its products help the players to better prepare themselves. Adidas and Seiko, in their advertising, show a group of players wearing the official kit of AC Milan and FC Barcelona, respectively, and Wayne Rooney features in advertising for EA Sports, alone and wearing an official Manchester United polo shirt (official image rights).

We can therefore identify three **types of players' image rights** that can be sold by sports marketers.

❶ Group official image rights. When players wear the official clothing of their team, we refer to this as 'official' rights. The club or national side often have the right to use and commercially exploit a group image (to include **at least four** players) and they will have obtained this through each player's contract of employment or participation. In the previous examples, this would be the case for Adidas, Seiko and Continental's advertising, which includes a group of players from AC Milan, FC Barcelona and the Spanish national side, respectively.

❷ Individual official image rights. The use and commercial exploitation of the rights of a single player wearing the official clothing of his team (for example Wayne Rooney for EA Sports) requires a specific agreement between the team and the player. The player cannot commercially exploit his image in official clothing without the authorisation of his team and neither can the team use the image of the individual player, even when dressed in club clothing. Many teams include clauses in their players' employment contracts to define the specific situations in which the club is permitted to use the individual player's official image rights (which are then offered to the team's official sponsors).

❸ Personal image rights: when players (or coaches) wear normal clothes or use products that do not feature the distinguishing symbols of any sports property (e.g. Piqué for Nike or Mourinho for Braun). These rights are usually owned by the players themselves, who therefore have total decision-making power over how they are used commercially.

In the table overleaf we can see how rights intermingle among the major sports properties in European football.

THE RIGHTS COMMERCIALISATION MATRIX IN EUROPEAN ELITE FOOTBALL

Rights commercialisation matrix			Rights acquired				Contract
Seller	Buyer	Events	Advertising	Official group player	Player (personal)	Images symbols	
Player	Club	Sporting	✓	✓		✓	Employment contract
		Communication	✓	✓		✓	
		Advertising	✓	✓		✓	
Club	UEFA	Champions	✓				Release of rights in exchange for prizes
		Europa League	✓				
		Press confs	✓				
		Advertising		✓*		✓*	
National team	UEFA FIFA	Euro finals	✓				Release of rights in exchange for prizes
		World Cup	✓				
		Press confs	✓				
		Advertising		✓*		✓*	
Player	Commercial brands	Advertising			✓		Commercial contract
Club/ national	Commercial brands	Advertising		✓		✓	Commercial contract
UEFA FIFA	Commercial brands	Advertising		✓*			Commercial contract

* Rights cannot be used in relation to a single team; only in relation to several teams and always putting them on an equal footing.

This table shows the different models for selling and granting rights based on three types of contracts: an employment contract, a release agreement and a commercial contract.

As you can see from the top left corner of the matrix, there is a lot of 'internal traffic' of rights, in the sense that they are transferred between different sports properties for their own use, although normally their ultimate destination is to be sold to advertising brands (the bottom section of the matrix).

At this point, we should consider an important factor relating to rights acquired for group or joint use. This is the obligation to use the group rights for several sports properties in an egalitarian manner. So, for example, a team or national side that has acquired its players' official group image rights cannot recurrently focus on any single player when using this image commercially, as it would then have to negotiate this player's individual rights.

In the same way, tournament organisers that have been authorised to use the team's rights (official players as a group, images and distinguishing symbols) can under no circumstances use them (or sell them to a brand) individually. For example, a sponsor of the UEFA Champions League can only use the rights to the competition and to the participating teams at a particular stage and as a group. I remember when FC Barcelona won the tournament in 2006 and we had to take out an injunction against one of the UEFA sponsors to make them stop repeatedly publishing adverts congratulating the team, using (without the right to do so) the club's trademarks. But this sponsor would have been entitled to publicly wish the two teams in the final the best of luck.

Let's go back to the case of the beer brands and David Villa that we described at the beginning of this section. As you can see in the table below, there is an overlapping of rights, and each of the five brands is legally permitted to commercially exploit the sponsorship rights that they have acquired, both by placing advertising at events and by using their other rights. The important nuance to this lies in the fair use of the rights classed as 'group rights' or 'of joint use'.

OVERLAPPING OF BEER BRANDS' RIGHTS IN RELATION TO DAVID VILLA

Brand	Sports property	Advertising	Official group player	Player (personal)	Images and symbols
Mahou	David Villa	✓		✓	
Damm	FC Barcelona	✓	✓		✓
Cruzcampo	Spanish national side	✓	✓		✓
Heineken	Champions	✓	✓*		✓*
Budweiser	FIFA World Cup	✓	✓*		✓*

* Rights cannot be used in relation to a single team; only in relation to several teams and always fairly.

Advertising spaces with a life of their own

Having rights and placing advertising are meaningless and have no value if the sports property does not manage to translate that into a large-scale and high-quality impact for advertisers and sponsors. It is the mission of advertising spaces, the third leaf of our winning clover, to achieve this impact, and for that reason, managing this must also be high up on the sports marketer's list of priorities.

As I mentioned before, my initial capacity to influence FC Barcelona's commercial and sponsorship projects was seriously restricted by the exclusive rights granting of several key assets. As well as the fact that, in 2002, most of the club's rights and advertising spaces were in the hands of third parties, we were the only major club that had not yet set up LED hoardings. I have vivid memories of how, in meetings with the director of assets at the time, I fought to overcome his resistance. According to his theory, the electronic hoardings were taller than the standard ones and would negatively affect the view from the front row of the Camp Nou. Besides, some managers believed that the light and movement emanating from the adverts would spoil the normal view of the match from the stands.

But the advantages of the new system were obvious: high-impact, moving advertising messages that we could commercially exploit right up to the moment before kick-off (unlike standard boards that have to be printed or painted one by one). After much insistence, I managed to convince them to install the LED hoardings quickly, to feature at a few matches that very season.

The boards surrounding the pitch are one of the highest-value advertising media, because they create impact on TV during broadcast matches. Let's therefore draw up the list of a sports property's most important **advertising spaces**, linking them to the various types of events and activities.

❶ **Matches**
  ▸ **Pitch-side static and dynamic advertising.** The advertising spaces closest to the game action have the greatest value and media exposure. As well as the actual hoardings, another important medium is the 3D mats that surround the goal. This group also includes other significant spaces such as the fourth official's scoreboard and the benches.
  ▸ **Static advertising around the rest of the stadium.** Hoardings and other spaces, inside and outside the stadium, that do not generally appear on the TV broadcasts as they are positioned further away from the pitch.
  ▸ **Players' official kit.** Advertising worn by players is also one of the

most highly valued spaces, because of the constant close-ups on TV and the photographs repeatedly published in the press.

- **Big screens.** Normally, the only medium on which video is permitted in the stadium (and hence, commercials), although its impact is limited to the spectators actually at the ground.

❷ Training sessions
- **Static advertising.**
- **Official player's kit.**

❸ Press conferences and interviews
- **Backdrop.** The advertising board that is placed behind the person who is talking (and whose statements generate media interest).
- **Microphone.** Advertising on the actual microphone or on other objects (such as water bottles or drink cans).

❹ Direct advertising
- **TV slots.** Advertising on the sports property's own TV channel. Sports properties can also reserve slots for commercials during broadcasts (as part of their contract to grant TV rights) or buy them under more favourable terms than the advertisers themselves can.
- **Newspaper spaces.** Inserting advertising into the sports property's own press or getting spaces in other newspapers and magazines.
- **Official magazines.** Advertising pages made available to the sports property (as it owns the medium).
- **Website.** Advertising spaces on the official website.
- **Club replica shirts.** Advertising on the official club shirts on sale at authorised outlets and worn by supporters.

It is clear, then, when it comes to advertising spaces, that the sports marketer's goal must be to create high-quality advertising impacts, which in commercial terms will convert into high-value media exposure for advertisers and sponsors. In the table overleaf, I refer to the different kinds of impacts, based on exposure and reach. The most sought-after impact will be through TV and nationwide (or international, in the case of the major sports properties). The degree and quality of the impact (depending on viewing figures, readership or hits) will serve as the basis for calculating the economic value generated by the various advertising spaces, and the **return on investment** for advertisers and sponsors. And of course we mustn't forget that advertising results will also influence the way the sports property's positioning is perceived.

THE IMPACT OF ADVERTISING MEDIA

Events	Advertising spaces	Impacts (exposure/reach)	Value
Matches	Static and dynamic pitch-side advertising	TV/national Written press/domestic	★★★★★
	Static stadium advertising	Stadium crowd Written press/domestic	★★☆☆☆
	Official players' kit	TV/National Written press/national	★★★★★
	Electonic scoreboard	Stadium crowd	★☆☆☆☆
Training sessions	Static advertising	TV/domestic Written press/domestic	★★★☆☆
	Official players' kit	TV/domestic Written press/domestic	★★★☆☆
Press conferences and interviews	Backdrop	TV/domestic Written press/domestic	★★★★☆
	Microphone	TV/domestic Written press/domestic	★★☆☆☆
Direct advertising	TV commercial slots	Depends on viewing figures	★★★★★
	Newspaper spaces	Depends on readership	★★★★☆
	Official magazine	Depends on readership	★☆☆☆☆
	Website	Depends on web traffic	★★☆☆☆
	Replica shirts	Depends on distribution	★★☆☆☆

The ideal impact of advertising

❶ Shown on TV and at peak viewing time.

❷ The advert takes up as much of the screen as possible.

❸ The number of brands shown at the same time is limited and they are all high-level.

❹ The brands are shown in their complete form, are clearly visible and the advertising messages are easy to read.

❺ If it is at the ground, the stadium is full.

❻ The advertising is well-integrated with the content.

❼ It happens at a moment of celebration (for example, a goal).

When attempting to maximise the value of advertising impact, the job of the sports marketer is divided into three activities: (1) analysing the regulations; (2) production; and (3) identifying new advertising spaces.

❶ **Analysing the regulations.** More often than not, the way advertising is displayed on different advertising vehicles is regulated by tournament organisers, who lay down rules regarding the number of brands that can be advertised on a single medium, the maximum size of the advert, and so on. The player's match kit is traditionally the medium that is subject to the greatest level of regulations. The sports marketer should therefore study the guidelines published by organisers very carefully and follow the rules to the letter. Any infringement can incur costs and damage the image of the sports property if the media ever picks up on it.

❷ **Production.** In my five and a half years at FC Barcelona, the team played numerous home matches for the UEFA Champions League. At every game, the special atmosphere created by this competition was accompanied by interminable production meetings with UEFA managers in which, with regard to marketing, the correct placement of the advertising hoardings and the TV cameras were scrupulously checked. It was all stipulated in one of the numerous manuals published by UEFA, which set out the exact points suitable for advertising and for every last TV camera. Of course, the aim was to ensure the best possible advertising impacts for the official sponsors.

LOCATION OF TV CAMERAS. UEFA MANUAL. CHAMPIONS LEAGUE 2011/12

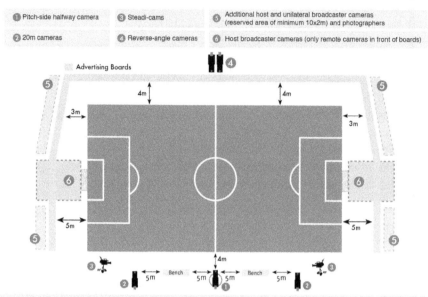

DIAGRAMME SHOWS STANDARD PITCH SET-UP. ALL DETAILS SUBJECT TO INDIVIDUAL STADIUM CONDITIONS.
Note: Pitch-side cameras to be positioned so that they do not present any danger to the players, coaches and match officials.

Any good commercial work the sports marketer may have done can be compromised if he or she has not paid enough attention to the advertising space production. A message that is too long, the inclusion of too many brands or decision-making based on live, visual perception of the advertising format (instead of thinking about how it will later be seen in the media) are just some of the mistakes that are commonly made. The sports marketer should therefore allocate some resources to production activities and work intensively on the following fronts:

▸ **Design of the advertising spaces,** making decisions on matters such as the type of technology used (for example, LED hoardings versus standard hoardings), the position of the chair where the person speaking in a press room will sit, the number of brands displayed on the backdrop (to which one must add the microphone and drinks bottles) and the location of the security staff.

▸ **Advertising design.** Given that the aim is to produce impacts that show the messages and brand names clearly and completely, it is vital that the right decisions are made about the design of the advertising. For example, the colour of the advertiser's logo should take into account the colour of the match shirt on which it will be printed; and there should be just the right amount of information to be easily readable. The sports marketer should work alongside the advertisers, who will normally try and insist that their logo is featured in their corporate colours and that sub-brands and slogans are retained, when they may not actually be very visible. In September 2012, I was struck by something that was much talked about among industry professionals: the small size of Gazprom's logo on the first advertising hoardings that this Russian energy company had designed as a brand new sponsor of the UEFA Champions League. The brand could hardly be identified in the TV broadcasts and this immediately elicited a reaction from the sports marketers (I don't know if they were with UEFA or with Gazprom), who then rolled out a new hoarding design with a much larger logo for the following matches.

▶ **Influencing camera positions.** Although photographers and cameramen do not generally appreciate being shown the exact spot they must occupy, at events organised by the sports property (press conferences, for example), the sports marketer has to do everything in their power to position the cameras in the place that will give the best advertising coverage. Remember that, however well-designed and well-positioned a backdrop is, if the cameras don't pick up the advertising behind the speaker at a press conference, all that design will have been good for nothing. It should be clear, then, that what matters is not what we see live at the event (the content that has been produced) but the advertising that is then shown on the media (the content that is reproduced).

Let's now take a look at some examples of how to manage advertising spaces production at different sports properties, based on how they are then shown on TV.

EXAMPLES OF HOW THE PRODUCTION OF ADVERTISING IS MANAGED

Badly designed backdrop

- Large logos prevent one from seeing the whole brand name
- Visually disorganised

Well-designed backdrop

- Maximum 6 brands
- Small-sized logos
- Visually well-organised logos

Badly designed backdrop   **Well designed backdrop**

❸ **Identifying new advertising spaces.** Ever since Emirates Airlines began sponsoring FIFA, at every trophy ceremony, some of its airline stewardesses appear in uniform carrying trays with the players' medals. At an event organised by FIFA, Messi was named 'Man of the Match' of the Club World Cup 2011 final and was awarded a stunning new car by the sponsor, Toyota. At UEFA Champions League matches, a child that has won a competition organised by Adidas gets to hand over the Adidas-branded ball that will be used in the match, to the referee. All of this, of course, is conveniently shown on the TV broadcast. The situations I have just described are good examples of new advertising spaces thought up by the sports marketers at FIFA and UEFA and they all help to add value to their respective sponsorship programmes. At FC Barcelona, we used to analyse the events produced by these sports properties in great detail, searching for ideas that we could replicate at matches in the Camp Nou. For example, we noticed that at Champions League matches, the players came out onto the pitch through an archway. We decided to put one up and include advertising on it at some games (we offered it to Damm for the one-match Joan Gamper Trophy organised by FC Barcelona, and to Audi when we hosted Real Madrid).

So, through observation, creativity and collaboration with advertisers and sponsors, the sports marketer should be constantly searching for ways to broaden the range of advertising spaces.

EVOLUTION OF OWNERSHIP OF FC BARCELONA'S ADVERTISING SPACES 2002–07

Evolution of ownership of FC Barcelona's advertising spaces		Ownership/control	
Events	Advertising spaces	2002	2007
Matches	Static and dynamic on-pitch advertising	TV3/Santa Monica	Mediapro FC Barcelona
	Static stadium advertising	TV3/Santa Monica Advertis (outdoor)	Mediapro FC Barcelona
	Official players' kit	Havas Sports	FC Barcelona
	Electronic scoreboard	ISO/Sony	FC Barcelona
Training sessions	Static advertising	Telefónica	FC Barcelona
	Official players' kits	Havas Sports	FC Barcelona
Press conferences and interviews	Backdrop	FC Barcelona (sold to Grupassa)	FC Barcelona
	Microphone	FC Barcelona (sold to Nike)	FC Barcelona
Direct advertising	Barça TV	Telefónica	FC Barcelona
	Official magazine	Godó/ADI	FC Barcelona
	Website	IMG	FC Barcelona
	Replica shirts	Nike	Nike

Coach's notebook

The sports marketer must achieve the production of large-scale, recurrent and high-quality advertising spaces through intelligent management of the existing advertising media, and the creativity and observational skills to identify new ones.

While it may seem like a hassle or a waste of time, it really is worth one's while taking a 'time-out' on the road to where the money is and finding one's way around the tangle of rights, working to reclaim those we consider essential and developing a portfolio of advertising media that is as broad as one can make it.

Maybe because of the pressure I was put under to get new revenue immediately, the first phase of my career at FC Barcelona was full of surprises (especially as I tried to sell assets that, unbeknown to me, had already been sold). I had not requested and carefully analysed all the contracts with implications for rights and advertising spaces.

Once I had all this information it became clear that, if its revenue was going to be able to increase significantly and consistently over time, the club would have to reclaim as many of the rights and spaces as it could. Through lengthy negotiations, the use of exit clauses that had been included in some contracts and by sacrificing short-term revenue, we managed to regain control in most cases.

SHOW ME THE TACTICS

❶ Assemble and analyse the following contracts:
  ► Players' employment contracts (you only need the clauses that stipulate image rights granted to the sports property and its sponsors).
  ► Contracts granting right to take part in tournaments.
  ► Sponsorship and advertising space sales contracts.
  ► Any other contract involving the sale of a right.
❷ Draw up an inventory showing the general availability and the owners of all the rights and spaces.

❸ Decide which rights and spaces it is important to reclaim and find out how much it will cost to do so.

❹ Check that neighbouring sports properties and their sponsors do not invade the territory of your sports property's rights.

❺ Comply with contracts and make your clients (especially advertisers and sponsors) comply with them too.

❻ Review the regulations for competitions in relation to placing advertising on different spaces.

❼ Visit the facilities at which the events take place and check the location of cameras (and try to influence this if possible).

❽ Gather examples of advertising impacts (TV images and press cuttings) and analyse the level of quality that has been achieved.

Goal assists

▸ Remember that it is vital that player's rights are available, if you want to sell sponsorship packages.

▸ If you are not able to buy back an advertising medium, consider the possibility of at least gaining control of it (for example, with clauses stipulating that they cannot be sold to sponsors' competitors) or of obtaining spaces for sponsors. The key advertising spaces to reclaim or control are the pitch-side static and dynamic hoardings, official players' clothing and press conference backdrops.

▸ Don't waste time reclaiming rights or media when there is no chance of succeeding.

▸ Ask permission from the TV cameramen to look through their lenses to see what the actual shots will look like.

▸ At press conferences, try to use tape to mark out the areas where you would like the photographers and TV cameras to stand so that the backdrop appears in their images.

▸ Analyse the advertising impacts that are achieved by other sports properties and assess their degree of success in order to get ideas on new advertising spaces and to work out which rights are being used.

▸ Seek out opportunities to swap advertising spaces with the media so that you can increase the range of advertising formats that you can use for advertising your sports property.

▸ Meet with the sponsors to identify new advertising spaces together.

▸ Keep the positioning of your sports property at the forefront of your mind in all your decision-making.

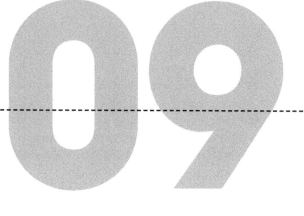

Selling
Sponsorship FC

Once we have a good commercial product, control over most of the rights and a wide range of well-managed advertising spaces (the three components of our very own 'winning clover'), we are ready to sell advertising and sponsorship for our sports property. All this is necessary, but not quite enough. In order to bring in that money and to keep it coming over time, the sports marketer has to have the right mindset and organisational skills, and to put in as much effort as is required.

In my first internal meetings at FC Barcelona, I used to hear statements such as 'We are Barça; anyone who wants to buy a hoarding or negotiate a sponsorship deal can come and find us. They know where we are and they just need to give us a ring'; or 'the vast majority of people who call are just wasting our time'. The attitude to selling was passive and reactive, and this was made worse by the team's bad results at the time: 'as long as the team is not winning, forget about selling anything', it was often said.

We have already acknowledged that sporting success is one of the sports marketer's principal allies, but this doesn't mean we have to sit and wait for it to come of its own accord. So, whatever the size of the sports property and regardless of whether the chances of sporting success are good or not, the sports marketer must approach the work of commercialising the sports property's principal assets with several particular attributes:

- **proactive sales mentality** – going out in search of potential clients with bullishness and determination, and responding to each and every phone call, even those that may initially seem to have little commercial potential.
- **well-organised manner**, using a methodology and prioritising tasks.
- **specific targets**, for both the short and long term.

Sponsorship and other forms of commercialisation

Now that we have come to our sports property's second main income stream, which in Chapter 2 we referred to as 'commercial and marketing', we are getting ready to make some money by commercially exploiting our rights to players, images and distinguishing symbols and by placing advertising in the various media available at each event that our sports property is involved in. We can do this in three ways:

❶ Block transfer of rights. Separate to the 'obligatory' granting of rights that has to happen if we want to take part in certain competitions, this model refers to the granting of all or most of the rights and media to a single company in exchange for a fee. This company then commercially exploits them by transferring them to brands wishing to advertise or sponsor.

❷ Single selling. The rights and media that are in themselves valuable can be sold singly to advertisers. Examples of this would be the sale of a certain number of hoardings or LED minutes during a match, or a space on the backdrop, and also the transfer of image rights for a player during a single event.

❸ Sponsorship programmes. Selling a set of rights and advertising spaces to a single client (the sponsor). These rights and media will help to forge a strategic connection between the sponsor and the sponsored sports property. So, unlike with the block transfer and single selling of rights, the sponsor is hoping that the attributes of the sports property will spread to their own brand in a natural and long-lasting way.

Sponsorship offers considerable benefits in comparison with the other forms of commercial exploitation. First, the time needed to allow these attributes to transfer across means that the contracts have to be of much longer duration, so the sports property is guaranteed more long-term revenue from a single contract. Second, the sponsor's use (or 'activation') of rights in its advertising is in itself a way of promoting the sports property and its sponsorship programmes.

The main disadvantage of sponsorship lies in the greater difficulty of identifying sponsors and, once you have, in the lengthy negotiation process, so usually the money arrives later, but stays for longer.

In my management role at FC Barcelona, I decided to drive aggressively the sale of sponsorship programmes before any other form of sale, although, as we saw, my starting point (with block and single-sale contracts in force) was a very complicated scenario.

COMPARISON OF FORMS OF COMMERCIAL EXPLOITATION

Forms of commercialisation	Block transfer	Single sale	Sponsorship schemes
Scenarios	• Overriding financial need • Availability of attractive offers • Requirement for tournament participation	• Financial need • Attractive advertising spaces • Transition periods (while in search of sponsors)	• Control of rights and spaces • Commercially valuable attributes by association • Attractive advertising spaces
Types of clients	• Intermediaries and specialist agencies • Tournament organisers • Advertisers	• Advertisers	• Advertisers
Clients' goals	• Financial profit • Brand awareness and sales	• Increased brand awareness • Increased sales	• Increased brand awareness • Increased sales • Transfer of attributes
Main competitors	• Other sports properties	• Other sports properties • Conventional advertising in media	• Other sports properties' schemes • Conventional advertising • Illegal actions • Ambush marketing
Recommendations	• Include buy-back clauses • Reserve spaces for sponsors (current and future)	• Short or long contracts with no exit clause • Do not sell to brands in key categories	• Long-term contracts • Choose active sponsors

In 2002, FC Barcelona had secured considerable sums of money as a consequence of contracts such as that with Havas Sports (block selling of sponsorship rights) and Santa Monica Sports. This latter company had the exclusive rights to commercially exploiting the static and dynamic advertising at every match in the Camp Nou (except Champions League matches). It had bought these rights from Televisió de Catalunya, the organisation that had actually bought them from the club along with the television rights.

As well as these block sales, key advertising spaces had also been sold individually to various brands. For example, the real estate company Grupassa had exclusively bought the backdrop, so it was the only brand that could feature in press conferences (along with Nike on the microphone). The sports newspaper *El Mundo Deportivo* also had a contract ensuring that its logo was the only one featured on the benches of the Camp Nou.

With the rights scattered around the place in the hands of third parties, it was physically impossible to set up a strategic sponsorship programme. So straight away we needed to design a process to reclaim them and buy them back, not forgetting that the group of block transfer and single sale contracts at that time made up the majority of the club's commercial revenue. Getting rid of this revenue overnight was therefore simply not possible.

Given this state of affairs, the most important decisions that we took at FC Barcelona when it came to forms of commercial exploitation were the following:

❶ Terminate the contract that gave the rights to sponsorship to Havas Sports. We negotiated this termination and, to avoid the short-term financial impact this would have, we agreed to pay back the sums we had received gradually at first, in the form of small commissions for some of the new sponsorship deals, even if those deals would not have been negotiated by Havas Sports.

❷ Reclaim the key advertising spaces, such as the press conference backdrop, the bench advertising and the website. In some cases, we got them back by not agreeing to renew contracts when they ended, even when in the short term this would lead to a fall in revenue. For various reasons, we never managed to reclaim the use of the static and dynamic advertising at the Camp Nou. So from Santa Monica Sports it went to ISO and then to Mediapro. Nevertheless, we did manage to insert clauses that allowed us to reserve spaces for the official sponsors (free of charge or at rates agreed beforehand) or even block out industries that might conflict with them.

❸ Design and roll out a sponsorship programme with the objective of, over time, having most of the revenue come from this source.

❹ Combine the sponsorship deals with the media sales to particular advertisers, as long as they don't occupy strategic advertising spaces for too long.

Competition and ambush marketing

To be assured of victory, one must identify one's enemies, study them closely and detect their weak points. Likewise, to get money out of a potential sponsor, we need to know who our competitors are and decide which weapons we'll use to bring them down.

It is no secret that when trying to attract sponsors, the sports marketer will come across plenty of competitors. The weird thing is that some of them may be from our own 'family' or might be strategic partners in other projects. So, for example, if we take another look at the overlapping rights in the beer industry that we studied in the previous chapter, this time from the point of view of FC Barcelona, we can see that, in practice, Barça's sponsorship programme is in competition with its own players' sponsorship schemes (in this case David Villa) as well as those of the Spanish national side, UEFA and FIFA. All of them are sports properties with which FC Barcelona has a strategic relationship.

The main competitors that the sports marketer will face in the fight for the money that companies earmark for marketing are:

▶ **Conventional advertising.** Advertising space offered by the media (TV, radio, press, the internet, etc.). This is sponsorship's biggest rival when the brand is only looking to increase brand awareness and sales (without any particular desire to take on the sports property's attributes).
▶ **Sponsorship in general.** Any other sponsorship programme, be it from another sports property or even from the arts, music or other sports.
▶ **Neighbouring sponsorship** of other sports properties in our area.
▶ **Unauthorised activities.** When a brand decides to use the distinguishing elements (name, trademark, logo, etc.) that have been registered to a particular sports property, in its own advertising with the purpose of associating itself to the sports property without having received the authorisation to do so.
▶ **Ambush marketing.** A common marketing term referring to a set of activities carried out by a brand with the premeditated goal of associating itself to a particular sports property, using in its communication, spaces, content and/or distinguishing features that differ slightly from the sports property's.

In 2010, Pepsi launched a global advertising campaign set in Africa with the participation of some of the best footballers in the world, including Messi, Kaká, Drogba, Lampard and Henry, with whom the drinks giant had deals to commercially exploit their personal image rights. In 2006, it had done the same with an advert set in Germany, with the participation of other iconic players such as David Beckham, Ronaldinho and Raúl. In both cases, the aim was simply to associate themselves with the World Cup tournaments in South Africa and Germany, organised by FIFA and for which Pepsi had no rights of any kind.

Both campaigns, developed by a world-renowned brand in a perfectly legitimate fashion, are fully fledged examples of ambush marketing. In them, Pepsi deliberately associates itself with the World Cup, but with a much smaller investment than that made by Coca-Cola, as the legitimate official sponsor.

EXAMPLES OF AMBUSH MARKETING ADVERTS

Advertiser	No.	Type	Aim	Rights used
Banco Sabadell	1	Partial ambush	Association with FC Barcelona	Pep Guardiola personal
Aliança	2	Unauthorised	Association with FC Barcelona	Barça trademark without authorisation
El Corte Inglés	3	Total ambush	Association with FC Barcelona	—
Halls	4	Total ambush	Association with FC Barcelona Association with *El Clásico*	—
Halls	5	Total ambush	Association with Real Madrid Association with *El Clásico*	—
Durex	6	Partial ambush	Association with FC Barcelona Association with Club World Cup	Victor Valdés personal
CAM	7	Total ambush	Association with Spanish national side	—
Prima	8	Partial ambush	Full association with Spanish national side	Spanish U21 players as a group/official
Mahou	9	Partial ambush	Association with FC Barcelona Association with Real Madrid Association with *El Clásico* Association with Spanish national side	David Villa personal Iker Casillas personal

EXAMPLES OF AMBUSH MARKETING ADVERTS

  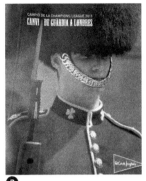

  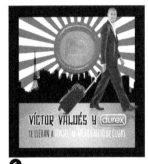

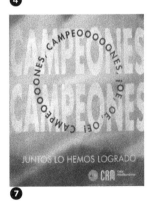  

1 'The biggest luck one can have is to do what you like doing. Finding that is at the essence of everything.' Pep Guardiola. (Banco Sabadell). **2** 'It's not just football. It's an emotion' (Aliança is much more). **3** Winner of the Champions League 2011. Changing the guard in London. (El Corte Inglés); **4** Pep, are you going to be needing one of these? (Halls). **5** José, are you going to be needing one of these? (Halls). **6** Victor Valdés and Durex are taking you to Tokyo, to the Clubs World Cup. **7** We are the champions! We are the champions! Together, we did it! (CAM bank). **8** Euro 2011. Let's go for it! Official Sponsor of the Spanish Under-21 Squad (Prima Juices). **9** Whoever loses, pays. Want to have a Mahou with Villa or Casillas? (Mahou beer)

We have just seen a list of examples of how different brands use the ambush marketing technique to associate themselves with a sports property without buying the right to do so. As you can see, I have distinguished between **total ambush** and **partial ambush.** So when Banco Sabadell hires Pep Guardiola, behind the objective of transferring the values embodied by this trophy-winning manager onto the bank's brand lurks another more ambitious aim: to transfer the values of the club he coached at the time of the advert, namely FC Barcelona. When Prima became the sponsor of the Spanish Under-21s, the underlying aim was to associate itself with the world champions; and when Mahou uses the personal image rights of two players it sponsors, David Villa and Iker Casillas, together in its advertising, as well as associating itself with the players and their respective teams, the beer company also manages to associate itself with *el clásico* (especially if the adverts are published around the time of the match) and the Spanish national side, of which both players are members. In all three examples, the advertisers have bought the rights to a lower level of sports property than they actually intend to associate themselves with. These, then, are examples of **partial** ambush marketing.

When the department store El Corte Inglés implicitly congratulates FC Barcelona (without using its name or distinguishing symbols) on winning the Champions League final in London, by showing a member of the Queen's Guard in a crimson and blue uniform, the aim of associating itself with the Catalan club is perfectly obvious. When Halls places adverts mentioning 'José' and 'Pep' in the Real Madrid and FC Barcelona sections of the press, what this manufacturer of sweets is attempting to do is to associate itself with the managers José Mourinho and Pep Guardiola, with their clubs and with *El Clásico*, and it does so without committing any legal offence, because neither of them have registered the names 'José' or 'Pep'. And when the Caja de Ahorros del Mediterráneo bank (CAM) congratulates itself on the victory of the Spanish national side at the World Cup final, using the colours of the Spanish flag, the aim is none other than to associate itself with the Spanish national squad. In none of these three cases has there been any rights acquisition, and this is why we can class these actions as **total** ambush marketing.

Finally, the use of the name 'Barça' in the advert put out by the hospitals and medical insurance company Aliança (example number 2) is a clear example of an unauthorised action.

Conventional advertising, sponsorship and, above all, unauthorised actions and ambush marketing present the sports marketer with a major headache. You will have to team up with the sponsors themselves to develop different strategies to highlight the advantages of a genuine sponsorship programme, and we will look at these strategies in later chapters.

Capturing sponsors, step by step

Signing a sponsorship deal comes at the end of a process that can take several months and that, as well as the sales effort, will require the sports marketer to use careful methodology and planning, so as to leave nothing to fate. That's because the desire and the urgency to have that money in your hand often translates into improvised, unstructured processes that can only lead to inefficiency. So by defining a method or process that can be applied repeatedly, you will be better prepared when entering negotiations on the terms and conditions of a sponsorship contract and will save time in the next rounds of sponsor recruitment.

Although I never considered it a methodology at the time, we did use a (more or less organised) process to secure sponsors at FC Barcelona. It was divided into four phases of action: (1) auditing and mapping; (2) designing the sponsorship programme; (3) producing the sales presentation; and (4) sales and agreements.

It resembles a stairway with four steps that one normally goes up one by one, but when in a rush, one can take two at a time. By this, I mean that when applying a particular work method (in our case, securing sponsors), one has to have some flexibility. In reality, the pressure to sell in my early days at FC Barcelona was so intense that we actually worked on the four phases simultaneously.

THE PROCESS OF SECURING SPONSORS

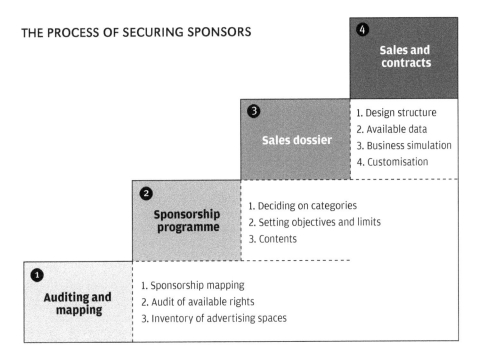

❹ Sales and contracts

1. Design structure
2. Available data
3. Business simulation
4. Customisation

❸ Sales dossier

❷ Sponsorship programme

1. Deciding on categories
2. Setting objectives and limits
3. Contents

❶ Auditing and mapping

1. Sponsorship mapping
2. Audit of available rights
3. Inventory of advertising spaces

Auditing and mapping

When, in 2005, Toyota told us that it was not going to cover the fee increase that we had requested for renewing its contract as the official car of FC Barcelona, we began the process of identifying a new sponsor in the automotive industry. And the first thing we did was to analyse the other major sports properties' sponsorship deals with car companies. So, from the outset, we ruled out Ford, Kia and Hyundai (the latter two from the same corporate group) because they were sponsoring the Champions League, the European Championship and the World Cup respectively. Given the massive investment required to sponsor any of these three global sports properties, we understood that none of them would have any budget left over to even think about sponsoring our club. So we opted to approach other brands. Real Madrid's success story with Siemens became the best sales pitch one could imagine when offering our sponsorship programmes to the competitors of this German company.

These examples serve to illustrate the importance of having a deep knowledge of the market and of the sponsorship activities of major brands and sports properties. So the first step on the stairway that will lead to us capturing the best sponsors requires some exhaustive analytical work from the sports marketer, focusing on three main areas:

❶ **Mapping of sponsorship programmes.** The idea is to draw an imaginary map on which you will position the sponsorship deals that your competing sports properties have in each key industry, as well as any movements that occur. One should also include any known details of the results of other sponsorship programmes. In the sales process that will come later, this mapping will help us identify natural candidates, rule out a good number of brands and have some good sales stories.

❷ **Audit of available rights.** In order to design a sponsorship programme, it is essential that the sports marketer has absolute and in-depth knowledge of who owns and controls the various rights that will be required. This audit, the consequence of analysing all the different contracts (mainly the players' employment contracts, the contracts granting rights in exchange for participation in tournaments and the single sale and sponsorship deals), will tell us if we have sufficient rights and what we can include in programmes and what we can't. By way of example, below we can see what might be the result of auditing the rights of Manchester United, assuming the level of competition it is generally in (participation in the Champions League).

AUDIT OF MANCHESTER UNITED'S SPONSORSHIP RIGHTS

Audit of sponsorship rights		Owner of rights			
Activity	Events	Advertising placement	Player's official/ group	Player's personal	Images Symbols
Matches	Premier League	Man Utd	Man Utd		Man Utd
	Champions League	UEFA	Man Utd		Man Utd
	FA Cup	FA	Man Utd		Man Utd
	League Cup	Football League	Man Utd		Man Utd
	Friendlies	Man Utd	Man Utd		Man Utd
	Training sessions*	Man Utd	Man Utd		Man Utd
Communication	Press conferences* Media events	Man Utd	Man Utd	Man Utd	Man Utd
Advertising	Commercials/ photos Media events		Man Utd	Players	Man Utd

* With the exception of those classed as official by tournament organisers.

❸ **Inventory of advertising spaces.** Our advertising spaces do not have unlimited capacity for advertising slogans and logos. That's why the sports marketer should have a detailed inventory of every single advertising medium at his disposal. This inventory should specify which spaces are already taken by advertisers and sponsors through transfer contract, single sale or sponsorship contracts.

In addition, the sports marketer needs to decide how many brands or advertising messages he or she proposes to include on each medium, because the more crowded (the greater the number of brands and slogans), the less value each impact will have.

In the table overleaf, there is an example that illustrates what the complete inventory of advertising assets held by a team participating in the UEFA Champions League might look like.

INVENTORY OF ADVERTISING MEDIA OWNED BY A TOP FLIGHT CLUB PLAYING IN THE CHAMPIONS LEAGUE

Events	Advertising spaces	League	Champions League
Matches	On-pitch LED minutes	50*	–
	3D mats	6	–
	Bottom stand hoardings	30	–
	Top stand hoardings	30	–
	Player's entrance arch	1	–
	Substitution board	1	–
	Centre circle (max. no. brands)	6	–
	Benches (max. no. brands)	4	–
	Electronic scoreboard • Fixed • Number of slots (20 secs each)	2 135	– –
	Stadium canopies/floodlights	100	
	Players' kit • Clothing brand • Shirt front • Shirt back • Shorts	1 1 1 1	1 1 – –
Training sessions	Training pitch hoardings	10	–
	Player's kit • Clothing brand • Number of brands	1 2	1 1
Press conferences /interviews	Backdrop (max number of brands)	6	–
	Microphone	1	–
	Bottles	2	–

Direct advertising	Official magazine	–	–
	• Full page	5	
	• Half page	15	
	• Back page	1	
	• Sponsors' joint page	1	
	Website		–
	• Fixed spaces on home page	6	
	• Fixed spaces in sections	12	
	• Banners (depending on hits)	,000	
	Facebook campaigns per month	10	–
	Mailings to databases per year		–
	• Normal post	12	
	• Email	24	
Players	Official group image rights (number of sponsors)	6	–
	Personal image rights (number of sponsors)	1	–

* Minutes effectively displayed on TV screen during broadcast.

With an in-depth knowledge of the competitive environment, a positive evaluation from the analysis of rights and an inventory of available advertising spaces, we are ready to climb onto the next step of the sponsorship stairway.

Designing the sponsorship programme

What criteria do we use to classify sponsors? How many categories of sponsors do we wish to have? How many sponsors do we want to recruit in each category? What do we give to each sponsor and at what price? These are just some of the questions that we were asking ourselves as we started to design the structure of the new strategic sponsorship programme at FC Barcelona in 2003. Besides the complex rights ownership situation that I've already described, we also had the issue of different criteria that had been followed in previous sponsorship deals, with the result that similar financial contributions had led to very different content. So, as with the design of the club's positioning, we opted to devote time and resources to designing the new sponsorship programme, bearing in mind that the resulting framework should remain in force for several years.

We studied the sponsorship programmes of the world's major sports properties in detail and were able to draw some interesting conclusions, of which I shall highlight three:

▶ Sponsors were arranged into categories. In the three or four main levels, most of the content was concentrated into the top two levels.
▶ There was never more than one brand from the same industry.
▶ The profile of the sponsors in each category was more or less similar.

In the table below, you can see the top three categories of sponsorship programmes used by some of the major global sports properties in the 2011/12 season. Although there are no shared criteria when it comes to the name given to each category, it is not too difficult to identify the different levels, both from the way sponsors are presented in general (for example, the size of the logos on the website) and from the perceived value of the content allocated to each of them.

2011/12 SPONSORSHIP CATEGORIES OF GLOBAL SPORTS PROPERTIES

Sport properties		Category 1	Category 2	Category 3
FC Barcelona	Name	Main partner	Premium partner	Official partner
	Number	2	5	6
Real Madrid	Name	Sponsor	Sponsor	Sponsor
	Number	2	5	3
Manchester United	Name	Official sponsor	Official sponsor	Official sponsor
	Number	3	9	13
Liverpool	Name	Main club sponsor Kit supplier	Official partner	Regional marketing partner
	Number	2	9	3
Juventus	Name	Technical+official	Sponsor	Sponsor
	Number	3	11	18
AC Milan	Name	Technical+official	Top sponsor	Premium sponsor
	Number	2	6	5

Bayern Munich	Name	Main sponsor Equipment supplier	Premium partner	Classic partner
	Number	2	7	13
Brazil National side	Name	Sponsors		
	Number	10		
Argentina National side	Name	Official sponsors	Official suppliers	Official collaborators
	Number	7	6	2
FIFA World Cup Brazil 2014	Name	FIFA partners	World Cup sponsors	National promoters
	Number	6	8	3
UEFA Champions League	Name	Official sponsor	Official supplier	
	Number	6	1	

When designing a new sponsorship programme, the sports marketer's first task is to decide how many categories or levels are going to be in it and how many sponsors we would like to have in each category. Throughout my career, the framework that I have most often used has had three levels and might look something like this:

RECOMMENDED STRUCTURE FOR A SPONSORSHIP PROGRAMME

Level	Category	Most important content	Max. no
1	Main sponsor	• Match shirt advertising (clubs) • Competition name (tournaments)	1–2
1	Technical sponsor	• Shirt sales • Match shirt advertising (clubs)	1
2	Official sponsor	• In-match advertising and at press conferences	5–6
3	Official supplier	• Supply of products and services to the sports property • Right to use distinguishing symbols	Unlimited

At FC Barcelona, we gave our top category to UNICEF (although it was not actually a sponsor as such; see page 31) and to Nike. In the official sponsors' category, we included our deals with Audi, Telefónica, Coca-Cola, Damm and TV3, and we decided that we would accept one more brand at most. These seven brands monopolised the most valuable rights and advertising spaces, while the other sponsors were classed as suppliers or official collaborators. Those categories included our contracts with companies that supplied the club (normally through barter agreements) and contracts of lowest financial value. Given that suppliers and official collaborators did not usually 'consume' our inventory of strategic advertising spaces and that they only had the right to use the distinguishing symbols and receive a small number of tickets for each match, we took the decision to set no limit on the number of brands in this category, which in effect was the 'bits and bobs drawer' of our sponsorship programme, but brought us significant sums of money (and cost reduction) without creating a sense of crowding. Finally, and because of the unique nature of FC Barcelona, we created a special category to include sponsors of the other sections of the club (basketball, handball, futsal, etc.).

Having defined the number of categories and sponsors, all that is left for you to do is to produce the document describing the sponsorship programme and establish a price policy. Taking the availability of rights and your inventory of advertising spaces into consideration, now is the time to define, in detail, the contents and quantities allocated to each sponsorship category. The sponsorship programme document should also include a section specifying the number of tickets that will be made available to each sponsor. In the next table, I have illustrated how to produce a sponsorship programme document. For the time being, it will be for internal use only, so the sports marketer does not have to devote too much time to the way it is presented. In fact, it may just take the form of a spreadsheet.

EXAMPLE OF A SPONSORSHIP PROGRAMME SUMMARY DOCUMENT

Type	Contents	Main sponsor	Official sponsor	Official supplier
Rights	Ownership, industry exclusivity and use of distinguishing symbols	Yes	Yes	Yes
	Right to shoot commercial with players	2	1	No
	Use of archive images in advertising	Any medium	Any medium	Excluding TV
Advertising spaces	On-pitch LED minutes	8	3	No
	3D mats	4	No	No
	1st/2nd level stand hoardings	6	3	1
	Players' shirts	Yes	No	No
	Training ground hoardings	4	2	No
	Stadium canopies	25	10	2
	Magazine pages	2	½	¼
	Database mailings	4	1	No
Tickets	Standard (per match)	50	20	4
	VIP (per match)	20	4	2

As you can see, there is no big secret behind the way one allocates content to each category. The idea is to reserve the most valuable rights and assign the greatest number of advertising spaces to the sponsors in the top levels of the programme because they are the ones that bring the most money into the sports property. So the allocation of media and rights should give rise to a visual landscape that is dominated by the sponsors that have made the biggest investments.

Talking about investment, we have left one important detail until last: the price of each sponsorship package. This is one of the most complex decisions that the sports marketer will face, because these prices can be extremely volatile and variable as a result of market shifts and the huge influence of recent sporting results. The following factors and situations may help to guide the sports marketer as they attempt to fix the **official price of a sponsorship package**, which will then serve as the basis for the negotiation process:

▸ Identify the combined price of the items on offer if they were bought individually (for example, advertising media and tickets).
▸ Research data relating to return on investment from independent reports (either commissioned by the sports marketer or provided by other sponsors).
▸ Find out what other sponsors of the same sports property are paying.
▸ Identify the prices paid by the sponsors of other sports properties (if this data is publicly available and reliable) of a similar profile and around the same time.

Rule of thumb for designing a sponsorship programme

❶ Be flexible. The sports marketer should use the sponsorship programme as a guide when it comes to the process of selling and implementing, but should be prepared to make changes to the general framework, the contents of each package and the pricing, as and when required.

❷ Prioritise. The availability of rights and advertising spaces changes over time. This rule of thumb stipulates that we should give priority to current sponsors over new content obtained through recuperation of rights or identification of new advertising spaces. The value of these items and our commercial relationship with the sponsor will dictate whether the new content justifies additional payments or not.

❸ Keep fair shares. Changes to the sponsorship programme (for example, increasing categories or brands per category and identifying new media) should respect the hierarchical levels that each sponsor has acquired in relation to the others, so their presence in the programme should not be 'diluted' unjustifiably.

❹ Limit activation. Sponsors at the lower levels should have limitations on their use of a sports property's rights and advertising (in terms of frequency and type of media used), in order to prevent them, having paid lower fees, from being perceived by consumers as having a stronger association with the sports property than the sponsors that pay most.

▸ Compile a specific business forecast arising from the sponsorship in question.
▸ Be clear about the level of exclusivity involved, both in relation to the number of industries and the geographical area under negotiation.
▸ Think about the intangible value of associating oneself with the sports property. The right to use its distinguishing symbols in the sponsor's advertising or to include the words 'proud official sponsor of …' in its advertising messages. Even if this is difficult to put an objective value on, it should still be considered an important element in the price. At times of sporting success, it can turn out to be a winning card up the sports marketer's sleeve, allowing you to win much more lucrative sponsorship deals.

The final economic value of a sponsorship contract will be the result of combining all these factors and the result of a negotiation process that we will discuss a little later.

We shall end this section by referring to four rules of thumb that the sports marketer should bear in mind when developing, and later updating, the sponsorship programme.

The top-notch sales dossier

On 16 November 2005, I attended a business meeting that was to be one of the most important of my entire career to date. That day, managers and executives of FC Barcelona had been invited to the world headquarters of Nike in Beaverton, Oregon, USA, to sit down with the top management of this American multinational to negotiate the renewal and improvement of the sponsorship contract that had linked the two organisations since 1998, and which was due to end in 2008. The agenda set aside two hours for us to present the status of the club at the time and to set out our proposals and expectations for the new contract.

To prepare for this crucial meeting, we had drawn up an 80-page presentation intended to impress the Nike executives with the transformation that the club had undergone thanks to our management and to describe how our future plans could help Nike to generate more business. So, under the title 'The Start of a New Era', the sales dossier included detailed and exceptionally well-organised information on the evolution of the club from a financial, media and social point of view, in most cases confirmed by independent reports. A large chunk of the document was devoted to explaining the team's high competitive level and the possibilities it had to win major trophies in the near future. I remember that we even used betting companies' odds to prove that FC Barcelona was the favourite to win the Champions League that season (which we did). The positive sporting results that were predicted were an excellent additional argument to justify the increased fee we were going to request from Nike, given the logical expectation of increased shirt sales that would come with the sporting success we were hoping for.

This example of the presentation put before Nike takes us to the third step on the stairway to our sponsor's money and it illustrates the vital need to have a high-quality sales dossier that will help to:

❶ Attract the attention of the potential sponsor, in the midst of an avalanche of dossiers received from numerous sports properties.

❷ Provide all the information necessary to be able to make an initial assessment on the interest of potential sponsors.

❸ Justify the sums requested in an objective manner.

The sales dossier, as an accurate portrait of a company, will not only be used for pitching to potential sponsors but also for (with a few tweaks) presenting the sports property at any other kind of business meeting.

The production of the sales dossier is, of course, the responsibility of the sports marketer and he or she will have to apply the usual dose of effort, planning and creativity to come up with a good document that should be **structured** around eleven different sections, as detailed below.

❶ **History and relevant information on the sports property.** How it was founded, trophies won, historic wins, home stadium, notable players, etc.

❷ **Positioning and theme of the project.** Detailed description of the positioning, including some kind of positive 'headline' or title that will help to contextualise the project and give it more personality. For example, 'The Start of a New Era' that we used in our presentation to Nike; or others in the vein of 'Together, We Can', 'Board the Express Train to Success' or 'We Need Your Help to Get Out of This Nightmare' (for a team that's just been relegated).

❸ **Media exposure.** Data on TV viewing, radio listeners and readership figures for the content generated in different media and programmes related to the sports property's sporting and communication activities. Description of our own media and its coverage (e.g. copies of official publications sold or numbers of unique visitors to the official website). Visual examples of media coverage, ideally with the presence of sponsors.

❹ **Critical mass.** Include the supporter numbers kit with all the information you have available on numbers of fans, followers on social networks, registered users and customers. Point out which databases you can offer the sponsor for them to use commercially and specify how it can be segmented.

❺ **Sporting objectives** (not applicable to championship sponsorship). Description of the squad, style of play and expected results on the pitch.

❻ **Detailed fixtures list for the season,** highlighting the most important events (such as matches with the number one rival).

❼ **General arguments in favour of sponsorship.** In every presentation, it is important to remember the three main benefits that a company can get from sponsorship: (1) increased brand awareness; (2) increased sales (more business); and (3) transfer of attributes. Given that sponsorship competes with conventional advertising for the marketing budget, it is important to emphasise the business that inherently comes with the sponsorship project and the value of taking on the attributes of the sports property. *These benefits cannot be achieved with conventional advertising.*

❽ **Components of the various options available.** This section of the dossier should include detailed information on the sponsorship programme that we have designed (as seen earlier in the chapter), although we will be using a more commercial language based on the benefits that the potential sponsor will obtain thanks to our sports property. So instead of using the three-part classification, we shall use one with four parts: (1) exclusive content (equivalent to 'rights'); (2) advertising (instead of 'advertising spaces'); (3) hospitality and events (instead of 'tickets'); and (4) business, where we shall give a description of the sales potential inherent in the sponsorship package that we are offering.

❾ **Support material.** In order to give the dossier more credibility and specific sales arguments, it is important to add information produced by reputable third parties (the content of which goes in our favour). Let's see some examples:
  ▶ Independent studies, such as the *Fan Survey* by Repucom (which shows the number of fans nationally and internationally), or any other published report or study that we may have conducted ourselves.
  ▶ Reports on return on investment, including the economic evaluation of the advertising impacts generated by our sports property through our various advertising media.

MAIN COMPONENTS OF A SPONSORSHIP PROGRAMME

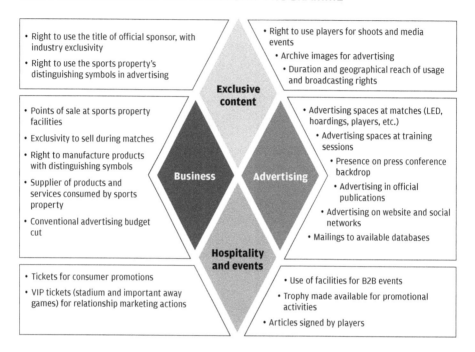

- Right to use the title of official sponsor, with industry exclusivity
- Right to use the sports property's distinguishing symbols in advertising

- Right to use players for shoots and media events
  - Archive images for advertising
    - Duration and geographical reach of usage and broadcasting rights

Exclusive content

- Points of sale at sports property facilities
- Exclusivity to sell during matches
- Right to manufacture products with distinguishing symbols
- Supplier of products and services consumed by sports property
- Conventional advertising budget cut

Business

Advertising

- Advertising spaces at matches (LED, hoardings, players, etc.)
  - Advertising spaces at training sessions
    - Presence on press conference backdrop
    - Advertising in official publications
  - Advertising on website and social networks
- Mailings to available databases

Hospitality and events

- Tickets for consumer promotions
- VIP tickets (stadium and important away games) for relationship marketing actions

- Use of facilities for B2B events
- Trophy made available for promotional activities
- Articles signed by players

▶ Case studies showing the results achieved by other sponsors thanks to our sponsorship project, in terms of return of investment, business development or transfer of attributes.

▶ Other reports commissioned by the sports marketer to meet specific needs. For example, I remember how we hired a specialist company in 2004 to help us identify arguments to counteract the perception held by many marketing directors that sponsoring FC Barcelona would lead to rejection by consumers in Madrid. Among other things, the report showed that sponsoring Real Madrid's shirts had helped Siemens to sell more and improve its brand image specifically in Catalonia (where the majority of FC Barcelona fans reside), which was, of course, an exceptional sales pitch at the time.

🔟 **Simulation of business potential.** Against this backdrop of widespread reduction to companies' marketing budgets, the chance to guarantee a greater volume of business for potential sponsors can become our passport to success. For certain sectors of sponsorship, it will be crucial to include in the sales dossier a forecast of the business that can be gained through our sponsorship, such as in terms of sales of official merchandise (for the sponsor that manufactures the kit), hotel nights potentially bought by the sports property for team gatherings or executives' trips (in sponsorship negotiations with a hotel chain), or food and drink consumption at the ground during matches. I remember how, when negotiating a contract renewal with Coca-Cola, the prediction of drinks sales at the Camp Nou (by dint of a sales exclusivity offer) helped us to close the 20 per cent gap we had in the negotiation.

⓫ **Executive summary and the main arguments.** Just as it is important to produce sales dossiers that are impressive in their size and content, it is equally (or more) important to provide an easy-to-access section

General tips on the sales dossier

▶ Avoid sending the sales dossier until there has been a face-to-face meeting, as you run the risk of it getting lost in an email inbox or among other presentations on the addressee's desk. Only in extreme cases (e.g. the impossibility of getting hold of the person you want to speak to) should you resort to sending it unsolicited.

▶ Customise the presentations whenever possible and as long as it's not too expensive to do so. Using Photoshop to simulate what the sponsor's logo could look like on your advertising spaces usually produces good results (as long as it is done with the right degree of quality).

▶ When the first meeting has been positive, try to produce and send a new version of the dossier, incorporating the comments received from the potential sponsor.

▶ Try to have the content and style of your sales dossier match the profile of your sports property. Even if you are really good at presentations, the idea is not to sell false expectations.

▶ Prioritise images and graphics over text.

▶ Always cite the source of the data you have included and use up-to-date information.

▶ Avoid including any confidential information in the dossier.

▶ Use the data you have available in a manner that is most favourable to you, but without manipulating the information (for example, growth figures instead of absolute figures).

▶ Avoid producing sales dossiers that are excessively large files (in terms of MBs) as this will make them hard to send and resend.

(at the beginning or the end) that summarises the main features of the sponsorship in no more than three or four pages. This summary should also include the main arguments in favour of the sports property (ideally, as compared with others), and it is intended for the potential sponsor's top executives, who have less time to analyse information.

In all the sections that I have suggested for the sales dossier, I have (completely intentionally) left out any reference to the price of the sponsorship. My personal experience has taught me that it is preferable not to include it in the standard document, for two main reasons: first, for reasons of confidentiality and the risk of the dossier falling into the hands of a competitor; second, so as not to come in too cheap. In this sense, as I said before, the price of a sponsorship package is exposed to major fluctuations and is influenced by a range of factors. Also, by observing a sponsor's attitude during the presentation of the dossier, we can get very valuable information for when it comes to proposing a sum.

Here it is! The sponsor's money!

In late October 2006, without featuring in the photos in the media, I discreetly, but with great satisfaction, celebrated the official announcement of the new sponsorship deal between Nike and FC Barcelona. Because of the sums of money involved and its duration, it was the best sponsorship contract ever signed by a football club. Almost a year had passed since negotiations kicked off at that meeting at Nike's global HQ in Beaverton and, since then, vice-president Marc Ingla and I had had countless negotiation meetings and conference calls.

The celebration of a new sponsorship agreement, as I noted earlier, is the sports marketer's greatest moment of glory and it far outweighs the huge amount of work put in to following the roadmap to where the money is.

And so we come to the last step on our stairway to sponsors, and it's time to finish the job. We are now more than prepared to win big sponsorship deals for our sports property, but we must still remain vigilant in this final phase, that of negotiating and selling. So, in our usual organised way, we shall be following a process that is made up of four final tasks for the sports marketer to accomplish:

❶ **Selecting natural candidates.** To increase our chances of success when negotiating, it is vital to attack the right 'prey'. So it is now time to revisit our mapping and to develop a list of companies that, based on the market information we have, could be natural candidates for our sponsorship programme. This analysis should also include an evaluation of the situation of our current sponsors' contracts in order to identify any possibilities of increasing the fees, and a review of costs to find opportunities for barter deals (sponsorship rights in exchange for products or services).

The candidate for 'ideal sponsor'

❶ Carries out (or intends to carry out) its activity in the same geographical area as your sports property.

❷ The manager that makes the decisions on sponsorship investment is a supporter of your sports property.

❸ The values and positioning of the candidate and your sports property are aligned.

❹ The company has been involved in other sponsorship projects in the past.

❺ It has a bigger marketing budget available as a consequence of plans to launch new products.

❻ It has recently lost a strategic sponsorship deal against its wishes, so the budget it had allocated to another sports property is now available.

The resulting list should prioritise actions and the intention should be (although this will be difficult in most cases) to reach a final negotiation phase with more than one interested candidate for a single sponsorship package. In the hypothetical case that one has several companies competing for the same package, one should follow these selection criteria:

▸ Total fee to be paid (yearly sums and duration of contract).

▸ Company profile and how it fits with our positioning.

▸ Intensity of sponsorship activation plans (advertising in the media, using our rights and distinguishing symbols).

▸ The relative importance of our sports property in the candidate's sponsorship portfolio.

❷ Defining the general sales strategy. At the announcement of the new sponsorship deal with Gatorade for the 2011/12 season, the general manager of AC Milan, Adriano Galliani, declared that the club had managed to almost halve the total number of sponsors (from 50 to 28) as part of a rationalisation plan, the goal of which was to have fewer sponsors but each of them to have more value (the classic 'less is more' approach). The really interesting thing is that this goal was achieved alongside increasing sponsorship revenue by 45 per cent (which in the 2010/11 season meant €92 million). Clearly, if we were able to choose our ideal sponsorship portfolio for our sports property, we would opt for a similar model. To achieve this, our sales strategy should consider two alternative revenue streams:

▸ **Capturing the core sponsors** (categories 1 and 2 of our sponsorship programme) by applying the 20/80 rule, the goal being that a small number of companies (20 per cent) can bring in most of the revenue (80 per cent). The financial value of each of the contracts will be very high, so it is very likely that one will require a considerable period of time to put this model into practice.

▸ **Single sales to advertisers.** Given the constant need to generate money, during the process to identify big sponsors, we should of course be making one-off deals to sell rights and advertising spaces. This involves temporarily having to sign low-value, short-term contracts with brands whose profile we would prefer to avoid in normal circumstances.

We also need to decide the way to approach different scenarios arising from sporting results, especially in terms of the pricing structure (fixed and variable payments) and duration of contracts. The following table suggests an action strategy for four different scenarios when it comes to sporting results.

NEGOTIATING AND SALES STRATEGIES ACCORDING TO SPORTING SUCCESS

Sporting scenarios	Current situation (recent results)	Expectation of future success
Favourable	• Increase fixed payment and minimise variable payments • Contract duration as long as possible	• Accept variable payment even if you need to reduce the fixed one (as long as they result in a higher total sum)
Unfavourable	• Accept lower fixed payment • Short-term contract	• Accept lower fixed payment • Reinforce benefits not related to sporting success • Try to avoid being penalised for bad results

❸ Meetings and negotiations. If the selection of candidate companies has been conducted properly, your sale results now only depend on the maths and on probabilities. The more sponsorship programme presentation meetings you have, the more chances of negotiating and closing new deals. It's that simple. So the sports marketer needs to focus on:

▸ Maximising the number of sales presentations.
▸ Carefully preparing each meeting.
▸ Multiplying the number of second and third meetings to maximise the number of negotiations you have open at any one time.

Coach's notebook

Whatever the size of the sports property, the sports marketer will carry out their commercial work in a highly proactive manner, trying to maximise the number of sales meetings and meticulously preparing for each and every one of them.

❹ The letter of intent. We've reached an agreement. We haven't yet signed the contract but we've shaken hands over it and your word is your bond. For you, as a sports marketer, to be able to make this declaration as you enter your boss's office, there will have been many fiascos and failed attempts to confirm meetings with more candidates on the list, many presentations in which you were not able to arouse the interest of the potential sponsor, and lots of negotiations that did not come to fruition. At this point, all that remains is to have a document signed by both parties as soon as possible – a letter of intent – that includes a summary of the main terms of the agreement as a precursor to the contract (which is a fairly complex document that will take some time to draw up).

You had already brought money in by commercially exploiting the stadium, and now you have found some more through sponsorship contracts and commercial agreements. It is soon time to work at reproducing it, but our roadmap tells us that there is still some way to go and there are other unexplored paths to money. Let's crack on.

SHOW ME THE TACTICS

❶ Identify your main competitors when capturing sponsors, especially any traditional ambushers.

❷ Evaluate whether the distinguishing symbols of your sports property are sufficiently unique and how vulnerable they are to ambush marketing.

❸ Do your sponsorship mapping to identify sponsors' action patterns.

❹ Draw up a table outlining your sports property's rights situation (audit), as a result of your analysis of all the relevant contracts.

❺ Make an inventory detailing all the advertising spaces that you have and their capacity to display brands and advertising messages.

❻ Write the sponsorship programme document, emphasising the structure of categories and the maximum number of sponsors you will accept in each category.

❼ Produce a high-quality sales dossier.

❽ Write a list of the ideal candidates to be sponsors, specifying priorities and updating it regularly with the meetings you have and the negotiations currently under way.

❾ Review the list of your sports property's overheads and preselect suppliers that could be candidates for exchanging products and services for sponsorship programmes (hotels, airlines, telephony, energy, advertising, etc.).

Goal assists

▶ Capitalise on periods of poor sporting results to buy back strategic assets at low cost.

▶ Try to build good relationships with players and help them to understand the importance of their active and positive involvement in the events that require their presence.

▶ Avoid letting a conventional advertiser (a single sale) buy a strategic advertising medium for a long time.

▶ Try to get valuable reports for your sales dossier without having to pay cash for them.

▶ When presenting the sponsorship options to a candidate company, if in doubt, always offer the highest category.

▶ Think about selling naming rights only if it brings major revenue that justifies fighting to get it accepted by the press and the general public.

▶ Leave presentations to companies that have never used sponsorship till last, because they involve a double challenge (convincing them of sponsorship in general and of sponsoring our sports property in particular).

▶ Try to wheedle out any sum of money you can from a company, however small.

▶ Bear in mind any legal implications when drawing up your list of candidates (especially in relation to alcoholic beverages, cigarettes, gambling and betting).

▶ Do not refuse to go straight to signing a contract (as opposed to a letter of intent) if that is a feasible option.

▶ Keep the positioning of your sports property at the forefront of your mind in all your decision-making.

10

Image rights, TV and licensed merchandise

Having filled the tank with money several times now, freshly refuelled, you follow the instructions on your roadmap, which tells you that there is still some way to go and more money to bring in. By commercially exploiting players' individual image rights, television rights and official merchandising, you can complete the last section of this stage and explore a very unusual way of capturing revenue. And that's because, for various reasons that will be pieced together in this chapter, some lucky sports marketers are faced with the paradox of being able to bring in a lot of money without working too much to do so.

The prime time of image rights

When, in late 2007, I christened the first of my very own enterprises Prime Time Sport, I took my inspiration from the time slots in the TV schedules that get the biggest viewing figures. In advertising jargon, this evening window is considered to be the place for the really 'beefy' content, so the cost of placing commercials is as high as it can be.

To calculate the commercial possibilities offered by players' image rights, we need to bear in mind that only a few players from each country are the focal point for most of the revenue potential, so in a sense they are equivalent to prime time television. In other words, very few sports marketers will be able to revel in the chance to get some good money from commercially exploiting image rights.

The market for personal image rights (those that do not use the distinguishing symbols of any other sports property) is made smaller by the consequences of players selling their rights to their teams and by the time spent playing football, so one can count on one hand the number of players with commercial potential.

TOP 10 FAVOURITE PLAYERS IN LA LIGA

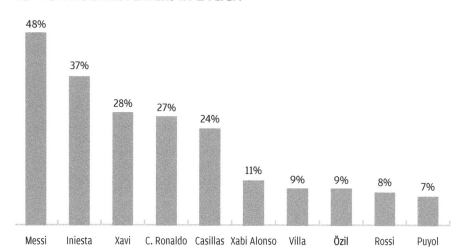

Source: Report produced by Ikerfel for the As newspaper, October 2011
Favourite players as voted per supporters polled

So the sports marketers that are in charge of commercialising the personal image rights of a player that is employed by a big club and plays for his national squad, that generates major and repeated advertising impacts by himself and that also has a personality attribute that stands out, have a big reason to celebrate. This celebrity player can help them to bring in a lot of money.

The VIP roadmap

The player is the smallest and therefore most vulnerable unit of sports properties. So although the sports marketer's roadmap is still perfectly valid when commercialising personal image rights, it will need a little tweaking to maximise the business opportunities for players who get a lot of media attention.

To find sponsors for an individual player, it's the associative content that gives the contract most of its value. So while other sports properties can get sponsors based on other items in their sponsorship programmes (such as advertising and hospitality), the sports marketer who works for a player has to take more risks when it comes to positioning and should therefore give it even more attention.

To give an example, I have developed a positioning map using five variables and in it I have placed four players who attract a great deal of media attention today (Cristiano Ronaldo, Lionel Messi, Wayne Rooney and Neymar). The result (purely for illustrative purposes but which should form part of the sales dossier) sets out major differences between these players

POSITIONING MAP OF TOP PLAYERS

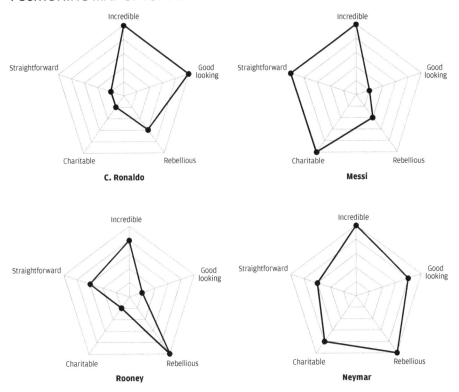

that will help the sports marketer to decide which variables (two, at most) will be used in the sales pitch with possible sponsors and to preselect the brands that best match these variables.

The next question requiring special attention is how the media exposure is managed. Although footballers can reap some benefits from the content distribution mechanisms that their team use (such as team press conferences or special reports in sports property media), it is highly recommended that a celebrity footballer has his own agenda and communication channels, in order to have greater control over the content that is published. All this has to follow the rules set by the team (club or national side), without having to use overly sophisticated or expensive channels (social networking sites can be sufficient).

Players' relationships with the media require organisation and planning, but also training. Issues such as how to dress, preparing for interview questions, the possibility of expressing oneself in different languages, the way to behave in interactions with fans, correct use of social networks or preparing an acceptance speech for receiving awards have a major impact in the positioning and media exposure, and they require the sports marketer and the player to work together. For example, at the FIFA award ceremony in December 2010, Messi was called to the stage to receive the Ballon d'Or (the main annual award for the world's best footballer), and he was so stunned that he didn't know what to say or how to stand in front of the microphone; a clear indication that he was completely unprepared. Neither did he acknowledge the runners-up, Xavi and Andrés Iniesta. The following year, he was awarded the same prize on the same stage and it was very obvious that he had prepared his appearance together with his advisers, with a speech that included thanks and a special dedication to his team-mate Xavi, who had been nominated once again.

Finally, the VIP roadmap also suggests a few special actions to be taken during commercialisation and the process to attract sponsors. First, we have the choice of sportswear, not just because this is the sponsor that brings the most cash but also because its use of his image has a decisive influence on the player's positioning and can be extremely useful for leveraging the recruitment of new sponsors. Second, one has to draw up a list of convincing arguments regarding the benefits of sponsoring a player as opposed to other categories of sports properties, given that there is widespread reticence among brands to link themselves to a single player. So in sales presentations, the sports marketer will have to highlight arguments such as that it is cheaper to sponsor a player and it allows one to associate oneself with more specific attributes.

The purpose of this is to counteract the general perception among brand executives that buying the image of a player is more risky, because of the risk of injuries or situations in his private life that can harm his image and negatively influence his performance.

The upheaval in the European television market

The evolution of the television rights market is one of the main examples of the spectacularly dynamic nature of the sports industry and it presents a massive adaptation challenge to sports marketers, who need to learn to deal with a huge array of different situations. For example, while some sports marketers claim that revenue from TV rights is their sports property's main income stream and they hardly need to take any action in this regard, others struggle desperately to even get their matches broadcast free on any TV channel to at least offer their sponsors some media exposure.

The UEFA Champions League increased its revenue from TV rights by 36 per cent from 2009 to 2012, and earned €850 million a year from that source. The top five clubs in the Deloitte Money League together earned almost €730 million, with an average annual growth rate of 8.7 per cent between 2006 and 2012. The big global sports properties continue to experience major growth in their revenue from TV rights. This is due to a range of circumstances, including globalisation and, above all, the fact that it is generally now pay-TV stations that buy the rights, and they have been able to capture viewers by democratising match prices and introducing new technology to improve the viewing experience, such as high definition and 3D.

So most sports properties have succumbed to the economic clout of pay-TV channels. Only La Liga in Spain (which is forced to by a law passed by the government) and the major events organised by FIFA and UEFA (to promote football and also to comply with certain laws) still get free TV broadcasts.

FREE TV VS PAY TV

Rights	Sale format	Type of TV				
		England	Spain	Italy	Germany	France
Premier League	Collective	Pay	Pay	Pay	Pay	Pay
La Liga	Individual	Pay	Free view Pay	Pay	Pay	Pay
Serie A	Collective	Pay	Pay	Pay	Pay	Pay
Bundesliga	Collective	Pay	Pay	Pay	Pay	Pay
Ligue 1	Collective	Pay	Pay	Pay	Pay	Pay
Champions League	Collective	Free view Pay	Free view Pay	Free view Pay	Free view Pay	Pay
World Cup	Collective	Free view Pay	Free view Pay	Free view Pay	Free view pay	Free view Pay

The serious reduction in advertising investment in Europe (the main source of income for free view channels) and the proliferation of budget cuts at state-owned channels have drastically limited their ability to compete with pay-TV stations for the most valuable rights. With this state of affairs, the free view operators have even agreed to acquiring shared rights (thereby renouncing exclusivity of broadcasts) or even withdrawing from the bids.

In this context, the polarisation of football becomes even greater: a small group of sports properties continue to increase their revenue from TV rights, year after year, while the rest fight for a bigger slice of the pie to share in the collective sale format or simply to put matches on air without any hope of getting any revenue from it.

The consolidation of collective selling of rights

The sports marketer's attitude to TV rights must, above all, be pragmatic, because in general he or she will have very little room for manoeuvre and will depend on the decisions of third parties or on collective decision-making. So we need to know the answers to two key questions. First, is it imperative to transfer the rights to a higher authority? And second, do our rights have any commercial value or not?

Transferring TV rights to then be collectively exploited is becoming more and more common. For example, in most of the major European leagues (but not La Liga), clubs have contracts in which they commit to transferring their rights to the league, which then sells them on the market and eventually redistributes the profits, based on various criteria. In the case of the major international tournaments (such as the World Cup or the Champions League), the national sides and the clubs are obliged by contract to transfer the rights (not just of television but also of sponsorship) if they want to take part in the competition.

MODEL OF TV RIGHTS TRANSFER FOR COLLECTIVE SALE

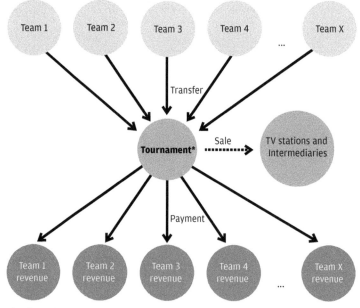

* Or higher-level sports property

It is precisely this agreement on how to redistribute the profit that is one of the main stumbling blocks faced by directors, to the point that in Spain (where FC Barcelona and Real Madrid hold most of the value) no stable collectivisation agreement has yet been reached, and in Italy the collective sale agreement was only achieved once a complicated mechanism had been designed to calculate the distribution. As a result, the move from individual selling to collective selling creates a diversion of money from the big clubs to the others. In the case of Italy, for example, it has meant an annual reduction in revenue of around €10 million for each of the biggest clubs (Juventus, AC Milan and Inter).

THE GAP BETWEEN THE BIGGEST AND THE SMALLEST EARNERS IN EACH LEAGUE

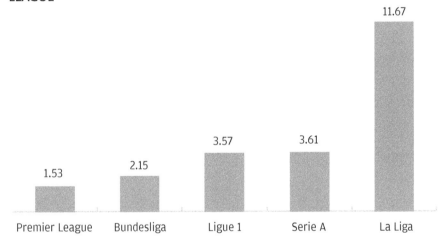

Source: Prime Time Sport

Data from 2010/11 (Premier League, Ligue 1 and Serie A) and 2009/10 (Bundesliga and La Liga)

To calculate the sum that should be paid to each team, all the following factors are generally taken into account:

❶ Equal payments made over time (Premier League, Serie A, Ligue 1, Champions League, World Cup).
❷ Sporting results (Premier League, Serie A, Bundesliga, Champions League, World Cup).
❸ Sporting results from previous years (Serie A, Ligue 1).
❹ Televised matches (Premier League) and viewing figures (Ligue 1).
❺ Fan base (Serie A).

181

It is also common in collective management of rights to keep aside part of the TV revenue to help teams in lower divisions and to promote grassroots football in general.

The next issue that the sports marketer has to resolve relates to the commercial value of sports property's rights, because his or her action plan will vary considerably depending on how valuable they are.

If the rights do not have any commercial value (a pretty common situation), the sports marketer will have to try to get his matches broadcast on some TV channel anyway, even if it is free of charge (placement strategy), in order to promote the sports property and achieve advertising impacts for the sponsors. If he or she doesn't manage to do so, the next step is for the sports property to produce images him- or herself and then try to distribute them on the internet and social networking sites (production strategy).

Finally, in the increasingly unlikely scenario that the rights do have commercial value and it is not necessary to transfer them in some way, the sports marketer will have the opportunity to freely sell the television rights on the market (selling strategy).

TV RIGHTS STRATEGIES

Commercial value	Goals	Strategies	Sports marketer's tasks
No value	✓Promote sports property ✓Advertising impact for sponsors	Placement	• Meetings with TV stations • Searching for sponsors
		Production	• Images production • Distribution on social networks
Has value	✓Financial revenue ✓Promote sports property ✓Advertising impact for sponsors	Transfer	• Influencing profit distribution criteria
		Selling	• Defining products • Contracts with intermediaries and commercialisation

Sensible commercial exploitation of TV rights

There are, then, only two scenarios in which sports marketers will have direct responsibility for selling television rights. First, those that work for federations and tournaments that receive rights transferred from other sports properties. Second, those with the opportunity to bring in revenue by commercially exploiting rights that have not had to be transferred upfront.

They all have a major challenge in common: they are expected to bring in large sums of money for their sports properties through negotiations that take place very infrequently (given that the contracts are of several years' duration and have the same start and end date for all the potential buyers). So a lot of their success will depend on sporadic processes that, although they are extremely intense, do not allow sports marketers to gain the experience they need to embark on the next process with any more guarantee of success.

This situation, along with the constant developments that take place in broadcasting technology and devices, and the ever more common presence of potential clients in other geographical areas, highlights the sports marketer's need to not confront this challenge alone, but to seek external help.

Coach's notebook

In certain commercial projects, the sports marketer should not baulk at seeking help from organisations and people with more experience and technical training, a larger portfolio of potential clients, and even the economic clout needed to be able to guarantee revenue and assume financial risk.

The only opportunity of any scale that I have had in all these years of taking part in a TV rights sales project came about at the end of my time at FC Barcelona. The process, led by vice-president Marc Ingla, resulted in the sale of all of the club's television and radio rights to Mediapro until 2013, for a total sum of almost €1 billion. Mediapro, who in a later negotiation extended the contract with FC Barcelona to 2015, had been buying up the rights of most of the teams in the Spanish Liga, including Real Madrid, and then selling them as a single product (Spanish La Liga) to TV channels all over the world.

So the business model that uses intermediary companies such as Mediapro consists of guaranteeing a minimum sum for the owners of the rights with the purpose of then selling these rights on the market to different channels for a higher total sum. Infront, for example, decided to risk €900 million per season in the form of a minimum guaranteed sum paid for the television rights of the Italian Serie A. It earned slightly higher sums (€911 million) for each of the two seasons that its contract was in force (2010/11 and 2011/12).

Intermediary companies are therefore a good support structure for sports marketers working for a global sports property, because they guarantee considerable turnover and can take you all over the world, which also promotes your sports property and provides advertising impacts for your sponsors.

Factors that determine the value of television rights

❶ The sports property's capacity to generate viewing figures time and again.

❷ Large crowds attending the live matches at the ground.

❸ Number of important matches.

❹ Rights packages: number of live matches, degree of exclusivity and geographical areas included.

❺ Regulation implications: if there is a legal obligation to broadcast matches on free view TV and if there are competition laws preventing one from selling all the matches to a single channel.

❻ Market factors: the number of channels interested in buying the rights.

Basic concepts in merchandising management

Working really hard to bring in just a little money doesn't exactly sound like a great plan to most sports marketers, but that is the risk that you face if the right decisions aren't made when it comes to merchandise and licence exploitation. As we shall see in this section, selling official merchandise can take up a lot of the sports marketer's precious time and resources, and it can hardly be considered the goose that lays the golden egg.

We shall start by reviewing the main definitions, requirements and actors that make up the landscape that the sports marketer has to manage. They are all generally organised around a licensing contract.

Merchandise licensing contract

An agreement by which a sports property gives a licensee the right to sell products and services that feature its registered trademarks in exchange for a financial payment (royalties).

❶ Sports property. This is the legitimate owner of the distinguishing symbols (trademarks, logos, badges, mascots, etc.). The business potential is strictly linked to the value of the commercial product (positioning, brand, media exposure and critical mass), as described in Chapter 5.

❷ Licensee. A physical or legal entity that acquires the rights to use the distinguishing symbols on its products through a licensing contract with the sports property. This entity is responsible for manufacturing and distributing the products (directly or through third parties).

❸ Distributor. The owner of the points of sale at which the end consumers can buy the licensed products. This is the licensee's regular client.

❹ Royalties. The mechanism by which the licensee pays the sports property, based on the volume of sales achieved by the licensee. It is calculated as a percentage of the price at which the products are sold to the distributor (not to the end consumer) and is normally around 10–12 per cent.

In order to familiarise ourselves with these concepts, we shall look at a breakdown of the cost of an official Real Madrid shirt made by Adidas and sold at the El Corte Inglés department store at a retail price of €75.

BREAKDOWN OF THE COST OF AN OFFICIAL REAL MADRID SHIRT

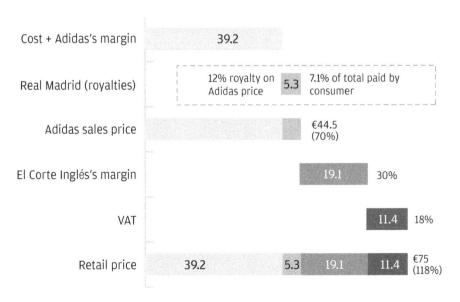

If we suppose that the royalty agreed between Real Madrid and Adidas is 12 per cent and, given that this should be calculated on the sale price to the distributor, we can see that for each shirt sold at El Corte Inglés, Real Madrid will get €5.30, in other words just 7.1 per cent of the €75 paid by the end consumer.

In this case, above and beyond the always welcome revenue in the form of royalties, what is of most interest to Real Madrid is the fixed sum obtained through the sponsorship programme that it has with Adidas. In fact, as we shall see a little later, the principal licensees of clubs and national squads are, indeed, their sportswear sponsors.

As you can see, the potential for direct revenue that a sports property can get from merchandising is, frankly, pretty limited. However, there are other objectives that mean that the sports marketer cannot afford to ignore this activity. For example:

▸ The need to offer business opportunities to sponsors.
▸ Improving the entertainment experience at the ground, which happens when supporters can wear their team's official shirt.
▸ Simply promoting the sports property.

RETAIL AND MERCHANDISING REVENUE AS PERCENTAGE OF TOTAL

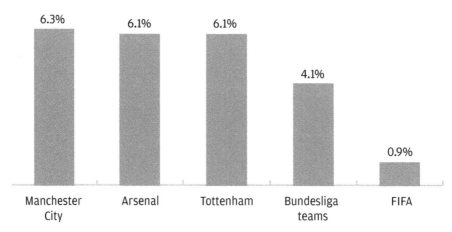

Source: Annual financial reports 2009/10 (Manchester City FC and Bundesliga); 2007/08 (FIFA); 2008/09 (Arsenal and Tottenham)

Outsource and conquer!

In its annual report for the 2010/11 season, Real Madrid revealed that it had licensing agreements with 120 companies selling official products, a not insubstantial number, and perfectly in tune with the size and scale of the club. This situation brings to mind my own experiences in this area, which were characterised by our sale of the retail and merchandising rights to Nike, due to begin in July 2002 – just one of the countless surprises that came my way as I took up my job at FC Barcelona.

I had hardly walked through the door of my new office when the general manager asked me to manage the transfer of all the licensed merchandise contracts to Nike, while I was trying to understand how the club had been able to sell something that I, not yet having any experience in sports marketing, considered really strategic. Jon Banks (my counterpart at Nike), and I sat down together and looked at dozens of licensing contracts in detail, many of them for small amounts or where the payment commitments had not been met. We invested a great deal of time in meeting with each and every licensee to explain our change of strategy and to manage the process of switching FC Barcelona's contracts to Nike. We found all kinds of companies, from big multinationals to small family businesses. I quickly realised that this comprehensive transfer of merchandising to Nike was not such a bad idea, so I took the decision to exclude merchandising from my personal list of rights that I had set out to reclaim.

So, sports properties can get money from merchandising by managing it in house (they can even become licensees) and by reaching agreements with third parties (outsourcing). While managing it yourself can help to keep more of the profit for the sports property, it does carry a number of disadvantages that make it a fairly unattractive option. They include:

- ▶ The legal and administrative workload needed to sign and follow up on a large number of contracts.
- ▶ Managing invoicing and checking sales figures to calculate the royalties.
- ▶ The sports marketer's need to devote time to the business relationship with all the various licensees.
- ▶ Lastly, if the sports property is acting as a licensee, it has to assume the financial risk and manage product stocks, for which demand is highly seasonal and volatile.

So as long as there are companies who are interested, the sports marketer should seriously consider the possibility of outsourcing as much as possible, thereby opting to do less work (and have more time for other projects) for more money.

If, on the other hand, the lack of proposals does not allow one to outsource the merchandising, sports marketers at clubs and national teams should identify the means of commercialising at least the official shirts, not just because of the business it brings but also as a service that must be offered to members and supporters.

REVENUE SPLIT FROM MERCHANDISING BY CATEGORY

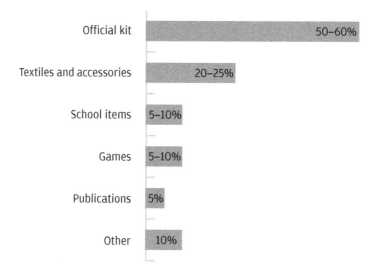

Let's now take a look at the various options when it comes to subcontracting or transferring merchandising rights and the circumstances that would lead one to choose one option over another.

When selecting the best companies to partially or totally manage merchandising, the sports marketer should conduct an even more exhaustive analysis than usual. Licensee companies will be able to present themselves on the market as strategic partners of the sports property and with complete legitimacy use its distinguishing symbols, not only on products but also on their sales materials. In the selection process, the following factors are just some of the ones that must be taken into account:

▶ The financial terms and conditions offered and the ability of the company applying to be a licensee to meet them.
▶ Previous experience in other merchandising projects.
▶ The relative importance of your sports property in the licensee's portfolio of merchandising products.
▶ The level of quality of the products to be licensed.

OPTIONS FOR TRANSFERRING MERCHANDISING RIGHTS

Type	Description	Circumstances for choosing
Licensee	• Exclusive licence to manufacture or sell a product (or category of products) in a country	• Categories or products of high consumption • Strong technical element – few options on the market
Master licence	• Exclusivity for more than one product or more than one country • Right to sub-license	• Low-volume groups of categories • Global sports properties for countries/small groups of countries
Exclusive partner	• Exclusive global agreement (all product categories all over the world)	• Need to relaunch brand and get results in the short term • Own staff not qualified • Sports properties with very infrequent events (e.g. FIFA World Cup)
Licensee sponsor	• Sponsor that also has rights to manufacture or sell licensed products	• Chance to get revenue from both sponsorship and merchandising
Retailer	• Licence to develop offline or online retail concepts with the sports property's brand	• Sports properties whose products are in demand all year • Online store • Home town and proximity to sports property's stadium

▶ The ability to innovate and to launch new products.
▶ The breadth of the distribution channel.
▶ The marketing plan proposed to drive sales.
▶ How the products fit with the positioning of the sports property.

The sports marketer's work is by no means over when the management of merchandising has been allocated in one of these formats (single licence, master licence, exclusive partner, licensee sponsor or retailer). In fact, the sports marketer should work with the licensees from the start to help maximise their sales, providing them with every possible means to do so (within reason).

During the selection process for FC Barcelona's official clothing for the 2005/06 season, Nike proposed two major innovations. The first was red shorts (instead of the usual blue) for the first kit and the second was fluorescent green for the away shirt. Nike also asked for our help in getting the team to wear the second kit when playing away, even if the first kit was not in the same colours as the local team. This was already common practice in England. With these innovations in the product design, and given that supporters want to wear articles that are identical to those worn by the players, Nike was naturally trying to achieve higher sales figures. After a sensible debate with the board of directors, we decided to approve these daring designs, which brought us a great deal of criticism from the media. The result was that Nike hit the highest ever sales figures with both the shorts and the away shirt, which translated into greater royalty revenue for the club. Futhermore, the FC Barcelona players went on to win the final of the UEFA Champions League 2006 at the Stade de France in Paris, wearing those red shorts.

On 30 July 2011, Real Madrid played a friendly against Leicester City, in which the Spanish team wore two different shirts (one for each half). With this decision, which in all likelihood did not feature as an obligation in any contract, the 'Whites' were attempting to help their licensee–sponsor, Adidas, to publicise the two new shirts for the 2011/12 season.

As we've seen in these examples, as well as the indisputably positive effect on sales of licensed products that come with sporting success, it is essential that the sports marketer work with the licensees to bring in as much money as possible from merchandising. This collaboration should happen in four different areas:

❶ **Product development:** the sports property must be willing to accept innovations proposed by the licensee.

❷ **Use of licensed products** by players and coaches.

❸ **Creation and legal registration of trademarks** and unique distinguishing symbols, giving the licensee all the instructions necessary for using them correctly (what is known as a 'style guide').

❹ **Anti-piracy actions.**

Red card for pirates

In late 2005, I received an email from a Barça member who was deeply shocked because while on holiday in Morocco he had found a shop that, under the name 'Boutique Barça', was illegally using the club's name and badge. Inside, one could also find numerous false products not just of FC Barcelona but of other major football clubs too. Having thanked the member for his information, I decided that the best thing was to do nothing because

EXAMPLE OF ILLEGAL USE OF DISTINGUISHING SYMBOLS

the cost of getting lawyers to take the shop owner to court would be infinitely greater than any benefits that would come from removing our trademarks from the shop.

While it is true that in many cases, the remedy is more expensive than the disease, we cannot ignore the fact that piracy is the number one enemy of merchandising sales, and that sports properties and licensees can together do a lot to fight it.

Let's highlight three types of actions that can be taken to try to control the growth of piracy, even if we can never eradicate it.

❶ Unique product design, using technology that is hard to imitate whenever possible.

❷ Frequent launches of new versions of the product that make the previous ones obsolete.

❸ Work with the police to track down large stocks of false products and give the items seized media exposure.

With the invaluable help of the very best guides (namely experts in TV rights and merchandising licensees), we can complete the most commercial leg of the journey to where the money is. In the next and final leg of the sports marketer's roadmap, the verb 'to sell' will make way for other, equally important verbs: 'to sign', 'to collect' (the money) and 'to renew'.

SHOW ME THE TACTICS

❶ Decide and define which of your own communication channels will be used by the 'celebrity' player.

❷ Draw up a plan for training the celebrity player so that he can get through even the most complex public appearances with flying colours.

❸ Make a diagnosis of your sports property's TV rights situation (if they should be transferred and if they have commercial value).

❹ Identify specialised external collaborators who can help you to obtain greater market value for TV rights.

❺ Decide which merchandising outsourcing model best meets the needs of your sports property among all the possible options: single licensees, master licences, exclusive partners, licensee sponsors, retailers, or a combination of two or more of these.

❻ Produce a style guide that sets out all the rules for licensees to use the distinguishing symbols of your sports property.

❼ Set up a formal procedure to approve new products from licensees and to check on their sales figures, which will be used to calculate the royalties generated.

❽ Work with the licensees to develop an anti-piracy action plan.

Goal assists

▶ Don't waste time looking for sponsorship contracts if your player is not one of the media's 'chosen few'.

▶ Base the positioning of your celebrity footballer in factors in which he scores highly, because average positioning does not help to differentiate him from the rest.

▶ Remember that if you open up an online communication channel (an official website, Facebook or Twitter account) for a celebrity player, you need to ensure that the content is constantly updated. It is better to have no presence at all than to have an ineffective presence.

▶ Even if the TV channel that has the rights for your sports property is not a direct client of yours, make an effort to treat them well when they are filming your matches. A good relationship and good service may come in handy for other projects.

▶ Try to sell your merchandising licensee additional sponsorship assets, to get greater overall revenue.

- ▶ Be sensible when hunting down piracy and only invest resources in making a complaint against large-scale cases.
- ▶ Don't get the jitters every time you see a false version of one of your sports property's products. Assume that you will never manage to entirely eradicate piracy; spend your time on other more valuable activities.
- ▶ Keep the positioning of your sports property at the forefront of your mind in all your decision-making.

PART IV

IMPLEMENTATION

Lawyer for a day

With handshakes, announcements and leaks to the press regarding initial agreements, or even agreements scribbled onto paper napkins, it is common in the world of sport to celebrate the successful completion of a negotiation process somewhat prematurely. But something very important is missing before one can truly celebrate success: putting down the details of this agreement into a contract, with all the rights and obligations of each party.

We shall be devoting the beginning of this fourth and final 'implementation' stage of our roadmap to looking at the basics of correctly formalising agreements into contracts. Although this may well be the least exciting part of the sports marketer's job description, careful and efficient formalisation will serve not only to make it easier to fulfil the agreements but also to minimise any risk of later conflict that may create an unwanted distraction. But do not fear, sports marketer: you won't need to swap your sports kit for lawyer's robes. Whenever funds allow, you will work with specialist lawyers to draw up and negotiate various contracts.

In this chapter, the key clauses that must be included in the main types of contract will be identified so you can begin to familiarise yourself with each of them. The complete structure and main clauses of a sponsorship contract will also be discussed, using a fictitious example hypothetically signed between an English Premier League club and a food product company.

The clauses that keep you awake at night

There are a number of clauses and elements in contracts that, because of their importance and how frequently they occur, the sports marketer must learn how to handle with perfect ease. They will become the centre of attention during the contract negotiation and drafting process.

❶ **General clauses.** Let's start by reviewing the clauses that feature in all contracts, of any kind, bearing in mind that the most important are probably those that refer to the financial terms, so that whenever possible we can secure payments with minimum hassle.

▶ **Financial terms.** The agreed sums, manner and date of each payment should be clearly stipulated. The sports marketer's goal, depending on how much bargaining power he has in each case, will be to ensure payment *whatever happens.* Particularly in today's economic climate, we must try to obtain bank guarantees (especially if we are working with new, relatively unknown companies) or, alternatively, make sure that payment date comes *before* the actual transfer of rights that has been agreed.

▶ **Duration of the contract and renewal mechanisms.** As well as specifying the start and end date of a contract, it should also include clauses that stipulate what will happen once the contract ends. Bear in mind that the client will normally try to get some sort of preference when it comes to renewing the contract on expiration. In this case, the sports marketer should try to get the client to agree only to an exclusive negotiation period for renewal and should avoid clauses giving first refusal and pre-emptive rights (by which the current client has the right to equal or even reverse the agreements signed with other companies on the same subject and with similar content).

▶ **Geographical area and industry exclusivity.** These clauses should describe, leaving no room for different interpretations, the geographical areas and business sectors for which rights are being granted, specifying whether they are exclusive or not.

▶ **Player participation.** In contract clauses that mention the use of players' image rights and player participation in events, it must be clearly specified whether this involves official rights (in club kit) or personal rights. These clauses should also include an exact description of the activities that players should carry out at events. The use of players should be planned as far in advance as possible, given their lack of availability due to the demands of the sporting calendar.

▶ **Approval of advertising materials.** Any contract must include a stipulation that the sports property approve all the activities and materials that involve the use of any of their distinguishing symbols, so that the sports marketer can check that they fit with the positioning.

▶ **Early termination of contract.** In contracts that grant strategic rights (for example, sponsorship of a team's shirt or television rights), it is recommended to include a clause that will allow you to terminate the contract in case of severe infringement (for example, not being paid), so that you can quickly regain the rights in question.

▶ **Jurisdiction.** In contracts signed with organisations in other countries or continents, the sports marketer will try to ensure that the contracts come under the jurisdiction of the sports property's country, with which they and their lawyers are more familiar.

❷ Sponsorship contracts

▶ **Sponsorship rights.** Include as much detail as possible in the description of rights, advertising space and tickets to be granted (measurements, location, exact quantities, etc.).

▶ **Costs.** The costs associated with implementing the contract that are to be met by each party. The sports marketer should try to get the sponsor to cover as many of the production costs as possible.

❸ Television rights contracts

▶ **Broadcasting commitments.** The strategic importance of media exposure means that it is a good idea to include a clause stipulating that the buyer of the rights has an obligation to broadcast coverage. The objective here is to prevent the channel that owns exclusive TV rights to decide not to air matches for any reason.

▶ **Production and transmission costs.** Unless agreed otherwise, the cost of production and TV signal transmission of matches (which are generally high) must be met by the buyer.

▶ **Commitment to display advertising.** The sports marketer must try to guarantee by contract that TV production of matches is done in such a way as to ensure that the stadium's main advertising spaces are visible, particularly when it comes to the LED system (or fixed hoardings) at pitch level.

❹ Licensing and concession contracts

▶ **Financial terms.** The sports marketer must do everything in his power to ensure that, as well as the royalties on sales achieved by licensees, payment also includes a guaranteed minimum sum. This item, which I highly recommend for projects with new licensees, will also act as a filter to identify the more financially solvent firms.

▶ **Sales checking system.** Regardless of whether a relationship of mutual trust is ever forged, it will be necessary to include a clause that identifies the system used to enable the sports property to check the veracity of sales figures reported by the licensee, which will act as the basis for calculating royalties. This system could, for example, entail the hiring of an independent auditor.

▶ **End-of-contract stock.** Any surplus stock on the market and in the licensee's warehouses can hinder the entry of a new licence on termination of a licensing or concession contract, as the new entrant will have a tougher time getting new licensed products out onto the market because they will be competing with the previous licensee's products. For this reason, it is a good idea to insert a clause into these kinds of contracts that lays down a limited period of time during which the exiting licensee can still sell and liquidate stock.

▶ **Product and service specifications.** Licensed products bear the sports property's trademark, so their specifications and quality parameters must be subject to the sports marketer's approval, by means of a dedicated clause in the contract.

Sample football club sponsorship contract

AN AGREEMENT made on the .... day of ...., ... between [the sponsor] of [sponsor's address], (hereinafter called 'The Sponsor') on one side and [club name] of [club address] (hereinafter called 'The Club') on the other side,

DECLARED
i   That The Sponsor is a renowned organisation that produces and sells FOOD PRODUCTS.
ii That The Club is a renowned sports club that currently competes in the first division of the English Premier League.
iii That both parties have reached the commercial agreements relating to sponsorship and to the terms and conditions stipulated in this contract which shall be governed by the following

CLAUSES
CLAUSE ONE. Purpose of the contract
By virtue of this contract, The Club appoints The Sponsor to be Official Sponsor of The Club and exclusive sponsor from within the FOOD PRODUCTS sector.

For its part, The Club, in exchange for the sum stipulated in Clause Six of this contract, grants The Sponsor all the sponsorship rights as described in Clause Two.

CLAUSE TWO. Sponsorship rights and industry exclusivity
From [start date] to [end date], the Club grants the Sponsor the rights identified below, as sole sponsor from within its industry, so that the Club cannot grant these rights either partially or totally to any other brand from with the FOOD PRODUCTS INDUSTRY.

2.1. Rights of association and contents

▸ Use of the title 'Official Sponsor of The Club' in The Sponsor's advertising, communication and promotional activities.

▸ The use of the titles, trademarks and distinguishing symbols of The Club in The Sponsor's advertising, communication and promotional activities.

▸ The Sponsor can use images of the facilities and players in its advertising, communication and promotional activities. The images must always be of groups of at least five players dressed in the official clothing of The Club, without giving any player more prominence than any other. These images shall be freely provided by The Club when owned by The Club or must be bought by The Sponsor from whosoever does own the rights to them.

▸ The Sponsor will have the right to film a television commercial featuring The Club, with the participation of its first team players. Filming will take no longer than three hours and should feature at least five players, all dressed in the official clothing of The Club and playing an equal role.

▸ The Sponsor can use the titles, trademarks, distinguishing symbols, images and commercials in any medium of communication (including but not limited to television, radio, written press and the internet).

▸ The Sponsor has the right to request 6 official Club shirts and 6 balls signed by the entire first team, per season.

2.2. Advertising

The right to place advertising at the following facilities (or others that replace them to the same end) and advertising spaces:

Stadium:

▸ 3 minute exposure on the LED system located between the edge of the pitch and the beginning of the stands, at first team home matches (whichever the stadium).

▸ 4 hoardings measuring 6 × 0.7m along the bottom stand.

▸ 3 thirty second advert slots on the electronic scoreboard (1 slot prior to kick-off, 1 at half time and 1 after the final whistle).

▸ The right to customise 4 gates into the stadium with strategic advertising for The Sponsor.

Training ground:

▸ 3 advertising hoardings, 5 × 1m, in an easily visible location.

Press room and mixed zone:
- ▶ Brand presence on backdrops in the press room and mixed zone, on which there will be no more than six brands.

Other media and activities:
- ▶ 3 pages of advertising per season in the official magazine.
- ▶ 100,000 banners per season on the official website.
- ▶ The Sponsor will have the right to send out 1 mailing, 3 emailings and 5 mobile text messages per season to the database of Club members. This will be done from the Club facilities and under no circumstances does it involve The Club giving The Sponsor any personal data, thereby complying with current data protection legislation.
- ▶ The right to distribute advertising materials at 3 matches per season.
- ▶ Brand presence, alongside other sponsors, on at least the following spaces:
  - ▶ Official photo of the first team line-up at home matches.
  - ▶ Official Club stationery.
  - ▶ Tickets and membership cards.
  - ▶ Tarpaulin outside the stadium.
  - ▶ Adverts for The Club.
  - ▶ Official team bus.
  - ▶ Homepage of the Club website.

2.3. Hospitality and events

For all matches played by The Club's first team at home:
- ▶ 4 seats in the President's box.
- ▶ 1 VIP box with 6 seats.
- ▶ 12 'class A' tickets with catering services included.
- ▶ 25 'class B' tickets.

For finals played by The Club's first team:
- ▶ All-expenses-paid trip with the team and complimentary tickets for two people.
- ▶ 6 'class A' tickets.
- ▶ The right to buy 20 tickets of the total number provided to The Club by the competition organisers.

The right to use Club facilities for The Sponsor's corporate events:
- ▶ A meeting room for a whole day, 6 times per season.
- ▶ The area surrounding the stadium for a promotional event, once per season.
- ▶ Tour by The Club's first team of The Sponsor's head office.

▶ The possibility of inviting 10 of The Sponsor's clients per season to watch a first team training session, with the chance to be photographed with the players.

CLAUSE THREE. Events included.

All matches, training sessions and media activities involving The Club's first team and directors and that take place at The Club's facilities (stadium, training ground and press room), with the exception of those for which The Club is obliged to grant the rights to a competition organiser (including but not limited to the UEFA Champions League).

CLAUSE FOUR. Geographical area.

The granting of the sponsorship rights included in this contract relates to [NAME OF COUNTRIES].

CLAUSE FIVE. Duration of the contract and preferential negotiation rights.

This contract will have a duration of [X] seasons and will come into force on the 1st July 201X and terminate on the 30th June 201X.

The Sponsor will be granted the first right to renew this sponsorship contract when it ends. The Sponsor can thereby be informed of and bid on any new conditions to be included in a new contract.

CLAUSE SIX. Financial contribution by The Sponsor.

As a fixed payment for the rights granted, The Sponsor will pay The Club the sum of £_____ for each season covered by the contract, by means of advance quarterly payments.

The Sponsor will also pay The Club the following sums as variable payments for sporting success: for the UEFA Champions League, £_____ for winning the tournament and £_____ for qualifying for the group stage; for the Premier League, £_____ for winning the tournament.

Should The Club's first team be relegated during the period of the contract, and assuming that The Sponsor would not choose to discontinue the contract, as described in Clause Twelve d), the fixed payment would be reduced to a third of its original amount for each of the seasons in which The Club was not competing at the highest level of English football.

VAT is to be added to all these sums at all times. From the second season, the CPI (official rate of inflation) of the previous twelve months will be added annually.

The sums will be paid net (i.e. free of commissions or taxes) to The Club's bank account [number _____] once all invoices have been presented.

CLAUSE SEVEN. Obligations of each party.

The Sponsor's obligations:

- To make all the payments specified in Clause Six in full.
- To request The Club's approval of any advertising and promotional materials that use the latter's titles, trademarks and distinguishing symbols, in the terms specified in Clause Nine of this contract.
- To use the sponsorship rights in good faith, always in accordance with current legislation and the regulations set by all the various authorities.
- To ensure that its directors, employees, representatives, partners and collaborators abstain from making negative comments about The Club and to prevent their behaviour from damaging the image of The Club.

Obligations of The Club:

- The Club undertakes to not enter into any sponsorship or commercial contracts with The Sponsor's competitors in the FOOD PRODUCTS INDUSTRY for the duration of this contract.
- The Club undertakes to allow The Sponsor to commercially exploit the rights it has been granted in this contract.
- Publicise the existence of this agreement between The Club and The Sponsor to the greatest degree possible.
- Abstain from publicly making comments or displaying behaviours that might damage The Club's image.

CLAUSE EIGHT. Costs.

Each party will bear its own costs that are incurred by carrying out the activities or meeting the obligations described in this contract, for example (but not limited to):

The Club will meet the following costs:

- Costs relating to the design and production of advertising and promotional materials shared by all The Club's sponsors (for example, but not limited to: stationery, tickets, membership cards, tarpaulins, Club website).
- The Sponsor will meet the following costs:
- The costs of designing, producing and maintaining the advertising spaces on which The Sponsor is featured as the only brand.
- The production and design of actions not included in previous paragraphs and any production or implementation costs they may entail (for example, but not limited to: leaflets, LED advertising at the stadium and hoardings at the training ground).
- Costs relating to the use of Club facilities for The Sponsor's events

and meetings (for example, but not limited to: catering, security staff and hostesses).

CLAUSE NINE. Approval of advertising.
Any advertising or promotional activity that The Sponsor intends to carry out using the titles, trademarks, distinguishing symbols and players of The Club will require the approval of The Club. This approval can only be denied (with objective and reasonable arguments) within a period of 7 days from the date on which The Sponsor's request is received.

CLAUSE TEN. Intellectual property rights.
The Sponsor grants The Club a non-exclusive licence to use the Sponsor's titles, trademarks and distinguishing symbols throughout the duration of this contract. This licence is limited to what is stipulated in this contract and The Club can only reproduce and communicate them publicly on advertising spaces and its own facilities.

CLAUSE ELEVEN. Confidentiality.
The parties undertake to keep the contents of this contract confidential and not to divulge them to any third parties, except in cases when obliged to do so by Law.

CLAUSE TWELVE. Termination of the contract.
This contract can be terminated for the following reasons, without prejudice to any compensation that may derive and any civil and/or judicial actions that may be entered into:
   a) At any time, by mutual agreement of both parties.
   b) In cases of serious infringement of any of the obligations assumed by the parties in this contract, without affecting the right of the injured party to choose to continue the contract and demand that the other party fully meet its obligations and repair the damages caused by the infringement. In particular, non-payment of the monetary sums set out in this contract, by The Sponsor, would be considered a serious infringement.
   c) If, for any reason, either party's core business no longer exists.
   d) On the request of The Sponsor, if The Club's first team no longer competes in the Premier League.
Should any of the circumstances outlined in point b) of this clause arise, the injured party should notify the other party, so that the infringement can be rectified within a non-extendable period of two weeks. If the party does not rectify the infringement within this period, the injured party has full right to terminate the contract without having to bring the matter to a Court

or Tribunal but simply by notifying the other party and providing evidence in writing.

CLAUSE THIRTEEN. Transfer of the contract.
The rights and obligations taken on by the parties to this contract cannot be either totally or partially transferred or subrogated by either party without the prior written consent of the other party.

CLAUSE FOURTEEN. Jurisdiction.
This contract will be governed by and interpreted according to English Law.

   In witness whereof the parties hereto have hereunto signed on the date written at the start of this contract.

Authorised by and on   Authorised by and on
behalf of The Club   behalf of The Sponsor

Signature   Signature

Full name and position   Full name and position

SHOW ME THE TACTICS

❶ Resources permitting, appoint a lawyer (internal or external to your organisation) to act as the person responsible for all contracts.

❷ Draw up a sample model for each type (sponsorship, licensing, etc.) so that you only need to enter the details and specific conditions that have been negotiated for each new agreement.

❸ Create a file containing the original copies of all the contracts, and keep it up-to-date and well organised.

Goal assists

▶ Try to ensure that it is your sports property that produces the first draft contract. This will give you greater control over the situation when drawing up later versions.

▶ In contracts of several years' duration, don't forget to periodically update the monetary sums involved to fit the Consumer Price Index (CPI).

▶ Remember to specify that payments should reach the sports property's current account free of bank charges (this especially applies to international bank transfers with currency exchanges).

▶ Always try to use the same lawyer so that you can build up a relationship of trust with them and so that it is the same person who pools the experience of most of the sports property's contracts.

▶ Remember that the information contained in contracts is highly confidential, so try to keep the number of people who can access them to a minimum.

Implementation par excellence

In March 2011, Dutch team PSV Eindhoven and Philips announced the renewal of their sponsorship contract for another five years up to the end of the 2015/16 season. There would be nothing unusual in this if it were not for the fact that during the period of this new contract, the two organisations will be celebrating nothing less than 100 years of collaboration, exactly the same number of years that have passed since the Eredivisie club (the highest football league in the Netherlands) was founded. The sponsorship includes highly strategic benefits such as the name of the stadium (the Philips Stadium) and the advertising that has featured on the shirt consistently since 1982.

This unusual case serves as an example to illustrate what one of the sports marketer's principal objectives should be: to get strategic sponsors to stay for as long as possible. A sports property with a high degree of sponsor loyalty (and therefore low sponsor turnover) reflects the fact that it has satisfied clients who – over time and through their advertising campaigns (using the rights of the sports property) – can become travelling companions on the sports property's road to where the money is.

The sponsors' level of satisfaction when I joined FC Barcelona did not exactly instil much optimism. The sponsors complained about a lack of attention from the club and some of them would tell me that 'they only call us when they ask for advance payments'. Therefore, improving and optimising the satisfaction of sponsors (particularly the club's most iconic ones: Nike, Damm beers, La Caixa bank and Coca-Cola) turned out to be one of my first challenges, particularly because we decided to use these four companies (with the later addition of Audi) as a launch pad for our new sponsorship programme. We got them involved in our strategic change plan for the club and we asked them to join us in this plan, as our travelling companions. We also asked them to be more committed to using their FC Barcelona rights in their advertising campaigns. Today, all the companies that were at the core of this relaunch plan are still sponsors of the club, following several contract renewals and fee increases.

Touch points in the relationship with the sponsor

It is clear, then, that the sponsors' satisfaction and success in their connection to a sports property should become one more obsession for the sports marketer. This connection generates constant opportunities to interact with the sponsor – 'touch points' – for which we should be aiming for the best service rating possible. We can use these touch points to describe what the ideal sponsor experience might look like during the three main stages of collaboration with the sports property: negotiation, implementation and evaluation of results.

THE TEN TOUCH POINTS FOR AN IDEAL SPONSOR EXPERIENCE

Negotiation	Implementation	Results
1 Sales dossier	**4** Advertising impacts	**8** Sponsor protection
2 Empathy between managers	**5** VIP treatment	**9** Information given
3 Announcement of agreement	**6** Sports property staff	**10** Feedback
	7 Priority for new assets	

1 Sales dossier. The first point of contact with the sponsor occurs at the initial meeting, when the document describing the sponsorship programme is presented by the sports property. The sales dossier should be properly structured, allow the readers to familiarise themselves with the characteristics of the sports property and clearly describe the benefits offered (exclusive content, advertising, hospitality and business potential). Ultimately, the dossier includes all the information needed to make an initial evaluation.

❷ **Empathy between managers.** Negotiations are held in an atmosphere of civility, allowing the potential sponsors to visit the sports property's offices. During the process, an empathetic relationship develops between the managers or directors representing each party.

❸ **Official announcement of the sponsorship agreement.** A public event is held to present the agreement to the media, at which the executive representing the sports property holds as high a position as possible. The announcement of the partnership gets full media coverage, including on television.

❹ **Advertising impacts.** The sponsorship project execution achieves regular press coverage with high-quality advertising impacts. As well as the direct advertising disseminated by the advertising spaces that form part of the programme, news coverage of the sports property's activities generates many additional impacts in the media for the sponsor.

❺ **VIP treatment at matches and events.** The sponsor receives preferential and exclusive treatment when attending sports property events such as matches (home and away) and press conferences.

❻ **Dedicated staff at the sports property.** The sponsor has access to members of staff that have been specifically assigned to the sponsorship project. These staff members are easy to get hold of, have time for the sponsor and are empowered to make day-to-day decisions on behalf of the sports property.

❼ **Priority for new assets.** New rights and advertising spaces that have been identified or reclaimed by the sports property are first offered to current sponsors, with or without additional monetary charges (depending on the value of each asset). Should the sponsor decide not to opt for any of the new assets, the sports property will still respect their industry exclusivity and will not offer them to competing companies.

❽ **Protection and anti-ambush marketing activities.** The sponsor has the peace of mind that the sports property's executives are protecting the integrity of their sponsorship (so that it will never become too diluted when other sponsors or assets come on the scene) and driving actions to counteract unauthorised campaigns and ambush marketing.

9 **Information given.** The sponsor is up to date with the sports property's activities, and regularly receives information on the advertising impacts that have been generated with the presence of its brand and any other report or relevant data that can serve to calculate the sponsor's return on investment.

10 **Feedback.** The sports property is always receptive to hearing new ideas and suggestions for improvement from the sponsor.

The sports marketer should constantly be working to create positive touch points, which, when taken together, give the sponsor a better perception of the sponsorship programme.

The sports marketer's renewal mentality

The colossal effort that is put in, step by step, from the auditing and mapping phase to the longed-for moment at which a new sponsorship contract is signed often causes errors of calculation at sports properties. The money is here, and the general sense of satisfaction may lead you to thinking that you have reached the end of the road. Nothing could be further from the truth. In fact, you are exactly at the midway point. So you, as a sports marketer, should be thinking that the distance travelled from the beginning of the commercialisation stage to the signing of the contract is precisely the same as the distance between this signing to the next contract renewal. But it is true that the final stretch is downhill and you will be depending much more on no one but yourself.

THE COMPLETE PATHWAY OF A SPONSORSHIP PROJECT

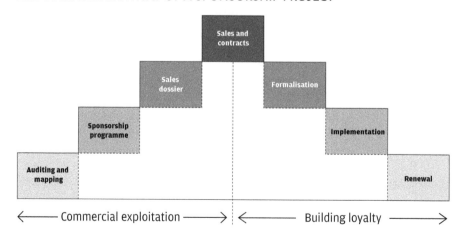

212

The renewal mentality is made up of six attitudes or ambitions that you should develop in your commitment to accompany the sponsor on the latter's own journey to a return on investment, knowing that the effort you put in can have positive side-effects in the form of attracting new sponsors.

Coach's notebook

From the very moment a new contract is signed, the sports marketer must start to think about renewing it and improving it as soon as possible.

COMPONENTS OF THE SPONSORSHIP RENEWAL MENTALITY

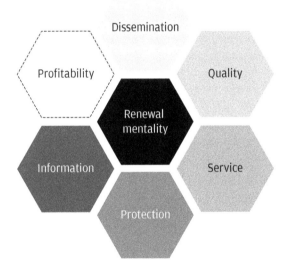

❶ **Commitment to publicity** and

❷ **Commitment to quality.** The goal of generating major, high-quality advertising impacts for sponsors is the first component of the renewal mentality. To meet this goal, the sports marketer must develop some of the strategies to disseminate content that we looked at in the chapter on media exposure. They include lobbying journalists, organising sporting activities and events, and buying advertising space from third parties. He or she must also prioritise production-related aspects such as the design of the advertising spaces, the design of advertising itself and the location of TV cameras. Other tasks will also need to be accomplished, such as:

▶ Selecting a person to manage the advertising spaces (the sports marketer him or herself if resources do not allow for this) – someone who is very au fait with the technical possibilities and limitations of each of them.

▶ Earmarking a budget to cover any advertising maintenance and placement costs that are to be met by the sports property.

❸ **Commitment to service.** For the sponsor to get the most out of the contents of the sponsorship programme, they will need to interact with the sports property constantly. Depending on the resources that are available and the level of sponsorship, the sports marketer should ensure that these interactions are to the sponsor's satisfaction and include tasks such as:

▶ Assigning a team member to act as the point of contact, so that the sponsor is always able to get in touch with the same person to deal with issues such as placing advertising, using exclusive content or receiving the complimentary tickets that are stipulated in the contract.

▶ Setting up a formal system to monitor the results of the partnership. This could be a monthly report, regular meetings or even the creation of teams (for large-scale sponsorship programmes).

▶ Handing over the sports property's distinguishing symbols and archive images so that the sponsor can produce their own advertising. They should be accompanied by all the relevant instructions to ensure that they are correctly used and reproduced.

❹ **Commitment to protection.** The sponsor also expects from the sports property that the latter takes action against unauthorised or ambush marketing campaigns conducted by companies also seeking to associate themselves with the sports property but by 'doing a runner' past the till. Some of the actions that the sports marketer can carry out to defend the legitimate rights of their sponsors are:

▶ Designing corporate advertising campaigns paid for by the sports property that legitimise the sponsors by including their logos (for example, thanking them for their support when celebrating a sporting success).

▶ Always creating distinguishing symbols that can only be used by legitimate sponsors. The design of these distinguishing symbols (logos and trademarks) should be unique and the symbols should be well-known by the public at large.

▶ Getting the media on board, asking your closest media organisations not to publish adverts that illegally feature your distinguishing symbols.

▶ Sending our legal requirements to offenders, demanding an immediate end to their placement of unauthorised advertising.

❺ Commitment to information. The goal is that the sponsor is always up to date with any of the sports property's actions that have any bearing on the sponsorship programme (in actual fact, this means most of its activities). As well as the information provided through the formal monitoring systems already mentioned, the idea is to share any studies, reports or results to which the sports property has access and to take the feedback received from the sponsor into account at all times.

EXAMPLES OF SPONSORSHIP IMPLEMENTATION

No.	Sports property	Sponsor	Type	Paid by	Description
1	Champions League	Heineken	Advertising	Heineken	Outdoor advert in Moscow to communicate association (commitment)
2	Ronaldinho	Lenovo	—	Lenovo	Company HQ decorated with player's image (commitment)
3	La Liga	BBVA	Advertising	BBVA	Advert to promote tournament and naming rights association (commitment)
4	David Villa	Maxibon (Nestlé)	Media coverage	Free	Free advertising impacts generated by an event
5	Real Madrid	Emirates Airlines	Media coverage	Free	Free advertising impacts generated by announcement of sponsorship
6	FC Barcelona	Turkish Airlines	Media coverage	Free	Free advertising impacts generated by sporting activity
7	Federazione Italiana (FIGC)	TIM	Advertising	FIGC	Advertising campaign to welcome new sponsor
8	FC Barcelona	Various	Advertising	FC Barcelona	Advertising campaign to celebrate titles with sponsors
9	AC Milan	Various	Advertising	AC Milan	Advertising campaign on sponsors' convention

EXAMPLES OF SPONSORSHIP IMPLEMENTATION

1

2

3

4

5

6

7

8

9

❻ Commitment to profitability. With a view to strengthening the relationship with FC Barcelona's main sponsors, in the summer of 2004 I took the decision to invite their executives and their wives to accompany us on the first team's 'friendlies' tour of Asia, despite the fact that none of the contracts set out any obligation to do so. The commitment to profitability consists precisely in constantly offering sponsors additional content that, at the end of the day, translates into additional profitability of the sponsorship project. Of course nobody is forcing us, but every time we give the sponsor benefits that are not stipulated in the contract, we are exponentially increasing their level of satisfaction and loyalty to the sports property. The sports marketer can achieve a lot very often and with very little effort: offer additional tickets; offer presence on new advertising spaces at no additional cost; get the players' involvement in the sponsor's events; use the sponsor's product in public; facilitate commercial relations among sponsors. These are just some examples.

SPONSORS OF FC BARCELONA, 4 AUGUST 2004, SHIZUOKA WORLD CUP STADIUM (JAPAN)

Marking the sponsor

The sports marketer's implementation work also includes a heavy load of 'dirty work' that cannot be left to one side. Not everything in our daily dealings with sponsors smells of roses. In many cases, the sports marketers will have to get out the cane and rap the sponsor's knuckles when they abuse the relationship or use the sports marketer's belongings incorrectly. Let's now take a look at some of the vigilance and control work that is also in the remit of our poor, hardworking sports marketer.

▸ Check that the sports property's distinguishing symbols are being used correctly on all of the sponsor's advertising and promotional materials.
▸ Approve the creative aspects of the sponsor's advertising campaigns when they centre on sports property content, so that they meticulously respect our positioning.
▸ Check that the rights to a group (of players or of teams) are being used in an egalitarian manner in the advertising.
▸ Bill the sponsor for the production costs that are not included in the contractual agreements.
▸ Ask that the sponsor meet the payment schedule agreed, if an infringement has occurred.

The work that relates to the implementation of sponsorship agreements comes at the final stage of your journey, and your roadmap has been very precise in guiding you here. It's been a long trip, which has not only taken you to where the money is, but also shown you how to take care of it and prepare the ground for it to grow and reproduce. With just a few more tips and final touches, the sports marketer will be ready to start a new journey, this time without the need for a guide.

The ten commandments for successful sponsorship

Content value
❶ Ensure repeated availability of crowd-pulling matches.
❷ Have the capacity to generate major advertising impacts, repeatedly and of high quality.
❸ Guarantee the value of the contents of the packages offered, especially in terms of players' involvement, the maximum number of brands accepted and rights granted to third parties.

THE SPORTS MARKETER'S ROADMAP

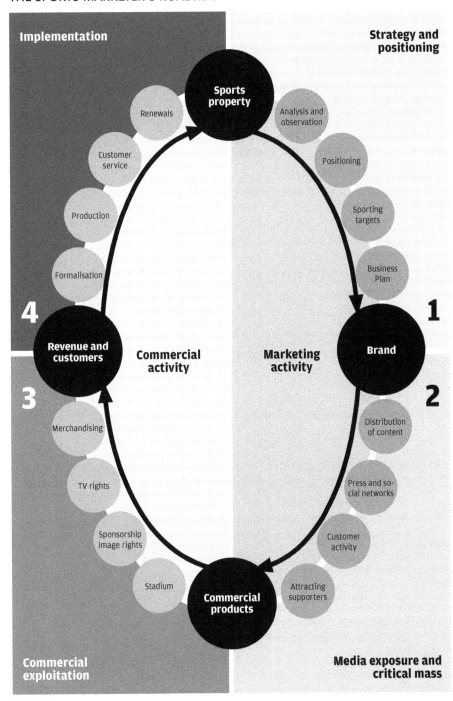

Commercial exploitation

❹ Sell a story or a project, not just a simple set of assets.

❺ Be assertive, to maximise the number of sponsorship programme presentation meetings and to be able to respond to any approach you get.

❻ Early identification of core sponsors that will act as strategic partners and travelling companions.

❼ Learn to sacrifice what looks like easy money, such as some single sell-offs, sales to brands with an unsuitable profile or sales to our sponsors' competitors.

❽ Provide objective data during negotiations and not just data based on predicted sporting success.

Implementation

❾ Build your sponsor's loyalty, implementing your contracts with excellence and with the commitment to offering more content than what is strictly stipulated in the contracts.

❿ Be vigilant and protect your sponsors' rights from abuses and meddling by other brands.

SHOW ME THE TACTICS

❶ Decide who will be responsible for managing advertising space and day-to-day interactions with sponsors.

❷ Ask for a permanent contact in the sponsoring organisation with whom to discuss any issues relating to implementation.

❸ Set up a formal and regular system of meetings for monitoring and approving your sponsor's advertising.

❹ Design both formal and informal systems that will give you data for assessing return on investment and sponsor satisfaction.

❺ Identify the sponsors that you want as your 'travelling companions' and share your decision with them.

Goal assists

▶ Let sponsors take part in most of your events, especially those that celebrate sporting successes.

▶ Try to build a personal relationship with the executives from your sponsors that are situated on the upper levels of your programme.

- Use all the parts of the renewal mentality in your sales pitch to potential sponsors.
- Don't waste too much time talking to the media and telling them not to publish ambush or unauthorised adverts because if they are important clients for these media organisations, they will not want to risk their advertising revenue.
- Keep the positioning of your sports property at the forefront of you mind in all your decision-making.

13

The proud sponsor

Having successfully followed your roadmap to the money, it is now time to complete your training. Then you will be ready to receive the final instructions to start the new season, which holds a plethora of situations and conditions.

The first thing this chapter will ask of the sports marketer (just once, and let it not set a precedent) is that you switch your tracksuit with that of the rival team, because this chapter will look at sponsorship activities from the other side of the negotiating table, requiring that you put yourself in the sponsor's shoes. The success of a sponsorship deal does not depend solely on the sports property. Some effective work on the part of the sponsor, working as a team with the sports marketer, is needed if we want to get the biggest return possible on the investment that has been made.

Sponsorship vs conventional advertising

The first issue that a company has to resolve when deciding on the feasibility of a sponsorship project is finding out what benefits it will bring compared with conventional advertising. We know that conventional advertising, depending on the execution, quality and budget, can give the company brand awareness and sales. But sponsorship can also bring the sponsoring brand a set of attributes held by the sports property.

The strategic goals of sponsorship
❶ Increase brand and product awareness.
❷ Grow sales and business opportunities.
❸ Develop association with and transferral of brand attributes.

The way in which the sponsor sets out the objectives will largely condition both the choice of sports properties and the sponsorship activities that will be implemented, bearing in mind that increased sales and brand awareness can also be achieved through conventional advertising in the media, without having to opt for sponsorship. But if association and the transferral of certain attributes do form part of the brand's strategic goals, sponsorship emerges as a unique marketing tool.

Activation, activation, activation

In June 2008, when the UEFA European Football Championship was going to be held in Austria and Switzerland, one of the main sponsors of the Spanish side was a client of Prime Time Sport. Given the positive outlook for success, we put to our client a proposal with a number of marketing and advertising actions to be executed if the Spanish squad did eventually come to lift up that trophy. The answer was unequivocal: 'with what we've paid the Federation in rights, there's no budget left for anything else'. On 29 June, Spain was proclaimed the champion, having beaten Germany in the final. The following day, most of the sponsors launched major marketing campaigns congratulating the team with adverts placed all over the media. At the end of the day, because of their more intense activation plans, sponsors that paid the Federation considerably less money for rights ended up scoring higher in terms of association with success and with the Spanish national side than our client did, in market research.

If the transferral of attributes does feature in a sponsor's strategic goals, we need to remember that it is a very good idea indeed to set aside at least the same sum as initially invested in acquiring rights, for activation. In this sense, sponsorship activation forms an essential part of a sponsor's action plan and that is why we shall be looking at it more closely later in the chapter.

Sponsorship activation

A set of commercial, marketing and advertising activities undertaken by a brand that has the use of rights obtained from a sports property through a sponsorship contract, to publicise them to consumers and achieve the other goals it has set itself.

The 360° action plan

The level of investment associated with sponsorship projects means that the sponsor has to work with the same kind of mindset as the sports marketer, putting in a great deal of effort, organisational skills and creativity. We shall be using the 360° action plan to organise every last detail of a sponsor's activities so that, as far as is humanly possible, the only piece in the jigsaw that will not be fully under control is the sports results of the sponsored sports property. The 360° action plan for a sponsorship project will be launched once the strategic goals have been set. It is organised into four phases: (1) analysis of opportunities; (2) selection and negotiation; (3) utilisation (or activation); and (4) measuring results.

❶ **Analysis of opportunities.** The marketing director of a company that aspires to sponsoring (or one of his or her colleagues) should draw up a list of the sports properties that are *a priori* most suitable for helping the company reach its strategic objectives. Any proposals received will be studied and others will be sought. Decision-making will be based on a number of criteria.

Criteria for preselecting sports properties
❶ Fees requested by the sports property.
❷ Market value of the advertising spaces included in the proposal.
❸ Level of presence in the media and capacity to generate advertising impacts for the sponsor.
❹ Outlook for the sporting results.
❺ Presence of other sponsors: degree of crowding and profile.
❻ Associated business opportunities.
❼ Critical mass of supporters and match attendance.
❽ Prganisational 'fit' when it comes to the following factors:
  ▶ Geographical areas of influence (current and future).
  ▶ Synergies in the calendar of initiatives.
  ▶ Brand positioning and attributes.
  ▶ Population segments.

❷ **Selection and negotiation.** The list drawn up in the first phase (which should not include more than three or four sports properties) should go through a second and final, even more demanding filter. By asking the sports properties for additional information (if necessary) or even commissioning one's own market research, the future sponsor can take the decision, based on a final, highly detailed analysis (due diligence) of the following factors and circumstances.

Due diligence regarding selected sports properties

❶ Degree of consumers' emotional engagement with the sports property.
❷ If there is any polarisation of feeling in a particular group of consumers (as a result of the way some sports properties are rejected by rival supporters).
❸ The sports property's vulnerability and attitude to ambush marketing.
❹ The availability and quality of databases.
❺ The level of service provided by the sports property to sponsors during the execution of contracts.

The result of this work of due diligence is that one will be able to choose the sports property with which to initiate negotiations to reach a sponsorship agreement. If in doubt about which sports property to choose, the sponsor may decide to negotiate with several candidates in parallel in order to get better conditions.

As an illustration, we can see below the hypothetical result of analysing various sponsorship options in the football world for a global brand.

SIMULATION OF A GLOBAL BRAND'S ASSESSMENT OF SPORTS PROPERTIES

Decision-making factors	FIFA World Cup	Champions League	National team	Top club	Top player
Financial investment	★★★★★	★★★★★	★★★	★★★	★★
Marketing and contents					
Risk of polarisation			★	★★★★★	★★★
Vulnerability to ambush	★★★★★	★	★★★★	★★	
Emotional engagement	★	★	★★★★★	★★★★★	★★★★
Sponsor crowding	★★	★	★★★★★	★★★★★	★★★★
Advertising					
Media exposure	★★★★★	★★★★	★★★	★★★	★★★
Spaces included	★★★★★	★★★★	★★	★★★	★
Continuity	★	★★★★	★★	★★★★★	★★★★★
Databases			★★★	★★★★★	★
Hospitality value	★★★★★	★★★★	★★	★★★★	★
Sporting performance risk			★★★★★	★★★	★★★★★

❸ **Utilisation of sponsorship (activation).** In October 2011, Banco Sabadell hit the nail on the head with a TV commercial in which the manager of FC Barcelona, Pep Guardiola, was interviewed by the Spanish film director Fernando Trueba. As well as the publicity gained from the TV ad placed by the bank itself, the declarations of the Barça coach on this commercial were picked up by all the big media organisations in Spain, so Banco Sabadell got a host of additional advertising impacts free of charge that were extremely valuable. One year earlier, the bank had celebrated the fact that it had attracted 15,000 new clients in just one month with its 'expansion account' (61 per cent of them from outside Catalonia, its main target). The advertising for this account was based on the image of Pep Guardiola. So from mid-2010 when Banco Sabadell managed to acquire the image rights of the Barça manager, its commitment and determination to activating the sponsorship was rewarded with a remarkable return on investment. Banco Sabadell has managed to squeeze out as much content as possible from its partnership with Guardiola, thanks to its comprehensive activation plan, which includes specific products, advertising, media events and direct or relationship marketing activities (the latter directed at its client base).

CONTENTS USED IN THE ACTIVATION PLAN

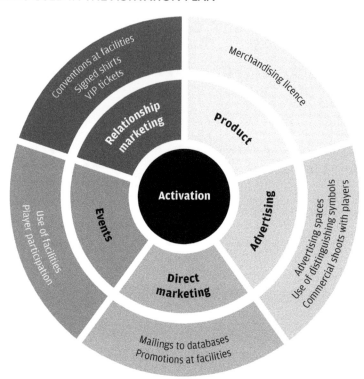

CONSUMERS' SPONTANEOUS RECALL OF SPONSORS OF THE SPANISH NATIONAL FOOTBALL TEAM

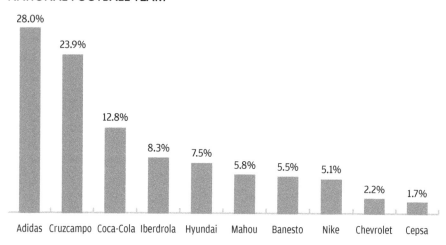

Source: Havas Sports 2010

Having signed the sponsorship agreement with the sports property, the third phase in the 360° action plan relates, then, to the activation of the sponsorship, where most of the sponsor's work is concentrated. The five main activities that form part of the activation plan make up a kind of 'marketing microplan' for the sponsoring brand, developed with the sports property's content. The illustration below shows us which of sports property content is used in the five groups of activities.

❹ **Measuring results.** After Spain's win at the FIFA World Cup in 2010, a report published by Havas Sports identified Adidas and Cruzcampo as the two brands consumers most associated with the Spanish squad. Interestingly, the report's top ten included no fewer than four brands that, without being sponsors of the world's winning team, had managed to associate themselves with it at the best possible time: the celebration of a major sporting success.

In the final phase of the sponsorship action plan, it will inevitably be time to take stock of the results, in relation to the goals that the sponsor had set itself. In other words, the moment has come in which to calculate the return on investment. To do this, the sponsor will be using three types of objective data:

Ⓐ **Sales and business.** In general and in certain geographical areas and sections of the population.
Ⓑ **The advertising value obtained.** The market value of the impacts obtained through sponsorship.
Ⓒ **Specific commissioned reports** to find out the association with the sports property and the transferral of attributes achieved in the eyes of consumers.

Just like the sports marketer, the sponsor also has massive challenges, numerous tasks to do and responsibility for big sums of money. The more knowledge the sports marketer has of the sponsor and his action plans, the more prepared he or she will be both for maximising sponsorship sales and for helping sponsors to achieve success.

We shall end this chapter by looking at some case studies, once again wearing our sports marketer's official tracksuit.

Case studies

In this section, we shall study a few sponsorship projects that stand out in particular, because of the effective strategy and execution work done by the marketing directors of various companies. The four proud sponsors that I have selected are Audi (football sponsorships), Nike (Champions League Final 2011), Coca-Cola and Mahou.

Audi

From the moment I joined FC Barcelona in 2002, I decided to try to get Audi to sponsor us. This German brand had an extremely stringent strategy for selecting sports properties and was already sponsoring Real Madrid in Spain. It was not until 2006, coinciding with our win at the Champions League final in Paris, that we managed to officially incorporate Audi into our sponsorship scheme. The massive sporting success was the final nudge needed to get the four-ringed brand (which also had to mitigate the 'polarised emotions' syndrome of its sponsorship of Real Madrid) to finally negotiate a sponsorship deal with Barça.

In the implementation phase, I was particularly impressed by how proactive Audi was. It had even hired an agency to manage all its activation plans. Following an exhaustive analysis of our facilities and advertising spaces, the first thing Audi did was to ask our permission to decorate the entrance to the players' car park with its brand images, since scenes of players driving into the club frequently appeared in the media. In this way, we created a new advertising medium for the sponsorship programme. The company also asked for our help in getting the footballers to drive Audi cars for private use, because this would give the sponsorship as much credibility as possible. When it came to the organisation of events, Audi was always meticulous about every tiny detail, especially if players were going to be involved. As a result, all the events got extensive media presence. We did have to devote a lot of time and resources to supporting the Audi executives, led by the marketing director at the time, Guillermo Fadda, but frankly it was worth it. We learned so much from them and it all helped to attract more sponsors further down the line.

Nike

When celebrating FC Barcelona's La Liga wins of 2004/05 and 2005/06 and the Champions League 2006, we had the invaluable help of Nike, whose marketing and activation strategy was notable in the way the company celebrated the sporting successes of its sponsored sports properties as though they were its own. In 2011, at the point when its sponsored teams, FC Barcelona and Manchester United, eliminated Real Madrid and Schalke 04, respectively, in the semi-finals, Nike was already the winner of the Champions League, even before the final that was yet to be played at Wembley. Nike's sponsorship of both finalists was an excellent opportunity to capitalise on success in advance, so the marketing executives quickly got to work. Using the slogan 'The Glory is Ours', Nike developed a global marketing campaign highlighting not only its sponsorship of Manchester United and FC Barcelona but also of some of the best players in both teams (including Wayne Rooney and Andrés Iniesta). With its usual impeccable execution, Nike created a comprehensive plan that included the following activities and more:

▸ **Product:** Nike started selling a special limited edition of the shirt worn by both teams in the final and also an exclusive commemorative shirt for FC Barcelona's victory, worn by players at all the celebratory functions.
▸ **Advertising:** Nike created a commercial with the players' involvement (it got more than a million views on YouTube) and placed ads in newspapers all over the world and on the main social networking sites. In London, where the final was held, a range of different outdoor advertising media were used, including special lighting of Marble Arch and canopies in the Underground.
▸ **Points of sale:** Nike Towns and the shop windows of various distributors were especially decorated for the occasion.

As a result of all this, and despite not being an official sponsor of the tournament, Nike managed to achieve all its big sponsorship objectives in a single campaign: brand awareness, business and being associated with success.

THE BIG SPORTS CLOTHING BRANDS AND THEIR CONNECTION WITH TROPHY WINS 2000–12

Competition	Nike	Adidas	Puma	Others
FIFA World Cup	1	1	1	—
Euros	—	4	—	—
Champions	6	6	—	1
Major leagues*	23	16	2	11
Ballon d'or	5	5	—	3
Total	**35**	**32**	**3**	**15**

* Teams sponsored in the Premier League, La Liga, Bundesliga and Serie A.

CASE STUDIES

❶ The clash is about to happen (Audi). ❷ For once, we want to see a spectacular crash (Audi). ❸ Passion leaves its mark again (Audi). ❹ Team enjoys go-karting without Mourinho. ❺ Valdés injured: doubtful he'll play Arsenal. ❻ Audi Cup 2011 kicks off.

1 The taste of victory. Congratulations, champions! (Coca-Cola). **2** Don't stop dreaming just because it's the fourth time your dream has come true. Congratulations European Champions (Coca-Cola). **3** Atleti visits Coca-Cola in search of some fizz. Club starred in brand's 125th anniversary. **4** Coca-Cola Cup. Ready to walk on the cathedral's grass? **5** Casillas has positive assessment of Mourinho's first year. 'I'd give the season an 8'.

Coca-Cola

In December 2011, the day *el clásico* was played at the Santiago Bernabéu between Real Madrid and FC Barcelona for La Liga, Coca-Cola managed to get free, widespread media presence thanks to a brilliant marketing initiative. Capitalising on its sponsorship of Real Madrid, the drinks brand prepared a wallet with two tickets for the big match and pretended that someone had lost it inside Real Madrid's official store. The idea was to see how supporters who found the precious wallet would react. The result (that most people decided to return the wallet) made headlines in the media and the originality of this marketing action was justly rewarded.

Coca-Cola's sponsorship strategy is unique in that the yearly investment of tens of millions of euros in its sponsorship of the FIFA World Cup (a global event) occurs alongside more local promotional actions like the one described above. Coca-Cola is one of the sponsors that I have worked with that most concerns itself with the 'polarisation of feelings', maybe because of the global nature of the brand. Because of this, when it sponsors football teams it does so by investing in rights and in a low-profile way, seeking mainly the business associated with the exclusive sale of drinks at events organised by the sports properties it sponsors. And when it does decide to carry out an activation campaign, it does so using geographical segmentation. Another important element in its marketing plan is also the Coca-Cola Cup, an annual grassroots football tournament it organises itself that traditionally obtains very good media coverage.

Mahou

The Mahou–San Miguel beer group's long tradition of investing in sponsorship projects (particularly the Mahou brand) is characterised by its goal of capitalising on the link with Spanish football and to be 'football's beer' in the eyes of supporters. Given that the strong competition means that it is not financially viable to sponsor all the football sports properties in Spain, Mahou has developed an interesting portfolio of sponsorships in which sponsorship plays a particular role in meeting Mahou's strategic goals:

- **La Liga.** Sponsorship of La Liga gives its advertising year-round exposure and helps to counteract the impact of Cruzcampo as the sponsor of the Spanish national side.
- **Real Madrid.** Allows it to exploit activation of the supporters' emotional engagement with the 'Whites' and dominate its natural consumer market, Madrid. It also brings business through the exclusive sale of Mahou at matches.
- **Atlético Madrid.** Helps to mitigate the emotional polarisation effect and reinforce yet further its dominant position in its natural market.

- **Iker Casillas.** The goalkeeper of Real Madrid and the Spanish squad brings Mahou additional content to activate, as well as an association with the Spanish side.
- **David Villa.** The player's transfer from Valencia to FC Barcelona was the icing on the cake for Mahou's portfolio as, along with the link to the Spanish side, it brought a connection to the Catalan club.

CASE STUDIES: TECHNICAL SHEETS

Audi	General strategy	Sponsorship of prestigious clubs with selective activation
	Sponsorships	Real Madrid, FC Barcelona, Chelsea FC, Bayern Munich, AC Milan
	Activation elements	Advertising, direct marketing, events, relationship marketing
	Aspects to highlight	• Association with prestigious attributes • Simultaneous activation Real Madrid and FC Barcelona to avoid polarisation • Product used by sports properties • Gets free advertising impacts • Identification of new advertising spaces • Fun events for players • Own annual tournament (Audi Cup, Munich)
Nike	General strategy	Sponsorship of prestigious sports properties excluding major tournaments
	Sponsorships	FC Barcelona, Manchester United, individual players
	Activation elements	Product, advertising, events , direct and relationship marketing
	Aspects to highlight	• Capitalises on sporting success • Gets free advertising impacts • Business associated with sale of commemorative shirts • Appealing advertising

Coca-Cola	General strategy	Sponsorship of major global tournaments combined with national sides and clubs at second level of sponsorship schemes
	Sponsorships	FIFA World Cup, UEFA European Championship, Olympic Games, Real Madrid, FC Barcelona
	Activation elements	Product, advertising, direct marketing, events, relationship marketing
	Aspects to highlight	• Activation is area-specific • Creative activation • Own annual sport event (Coca-Cola Cup) • Gets free advertising impacts • Exclusive sale of its product at sponsored events
Mahou	General strategy	To sponsor Spanish football
	Sponsorships	Real Madrid, Atlético Madrid, La Liga, individual players (Iker Casillas and David Villa)
	Activation elements	Product, advertising, events, direct and relationship marketing
	Aspects to highlight	• Strategic choice of sports properties that are key in Spanish football • Gets free advertising impacts • Opportunistic activation campaigns • Exclusive sale of product (Real Madrid and Atlético Madrid)

The ten commandments for the proud sponsor

1 The sponsor must clearly define the objectives that they want to achieve through the sponsorship, particularly in relation to conventional advertising.

2 The sponsor must carefully develop a strategy for selecting sports properties that can help to achieve its objectives.

3 The sponsor must make some of the sponsorship fee variable and linked to the sports property's sporting success and, wherever possible, to the sponsor's business results.

4 The sponsor must emphasise their future intentions for activation during the negotiation process.

5 The sponsor must exploit the sponsorship benefits to the maximum and only buy the content that they intend to use for activation.

6 The sponsor must produce the contents of their activation plan with excellence and creativity.

7 The sponsor must celebrate the sporting successes of the sports properties they sponsor by developing specific marketing campaigns.

8 The sponsor must build a friendly relationship with the sports property's executives and with its players.

9 The sponsor must get the media on their side in order to maximise free coverage of their activities.

10 The sponsor must set out a plan with the data and sources of information that will be used for measuring return on investment.

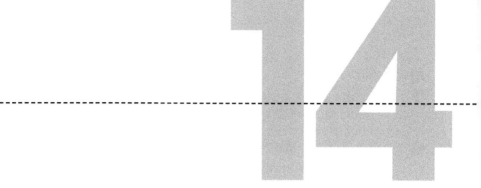

The 'Ballon d'Or' sports marketer

The preseason is over and you're ready to pep-talk the eleven players who will be walking out onto the pitch for the first official competition match. You know perfectly well that you can't win on your own, so you need to get the very best performance out of your players, with the invaluable assistance of your coaching staff. During the talk, you will pay special attention to the forwards and you'll share with them some of the tricks that helped you score goals when you were a player. You want to win the match and you want to win the Ballon d'Or for best sports marketer of the year.

The first eleven and the technical staff

I would like to use the metaphor of a football team formation to pay tribute to your principal team members and look at each of their roles, in the knowledge that in real life, in most sports properties each team member will have to fulfil two or more functions of those described below and, in general, you will be outsourcing many of the activities to avoid overloading your overheads structure.

In defence …
1 **Guardian of the brand.** The person responsible for designing, registering and controlling the use of trademarks and distinguishing symbols.

2 **Customer service.** The employees assigned to implementing agreements with sponsors and responding to requests from members and other customers.

3 **Finance.** The master of the spreadsheets that contain the accounts, the business plan and monitoring of the expenses budget.

④ **Advertising space manager.** Responsible for the upkeep of advertising spaces and correct placement of advertising for advertisers and sponsors.

⑤ **Content manager.** Production and supervision of content published in the sports property's own media (magazine, website, social networks, etc.)

Midfield ...

⑥ **Press relations.** Responsible for interacting with the media with a view to maximising the quantity and quality of published content.

⑧ **Data and reports researcher.** Their mission is to get as much information as possible (ideally free of charge) to include in the sales dossiers.

⑩ **The presentations whizz-kid.** The person who really knows their stuff when it comes to graphic design and can edit videos to provide truly spectacular sales dossiers.

Forward ...

⑦ **Ticket sales manager.** The person or team responsible for maximising ticket sales, sell-out matches and other stadium revenue.

⑨ **Sponsorship sales manager.** The goalscorer of your team – responsible for securing the presentation and negotiation meetings with interested companies and finally getting the agreements in writing.

⑪ **The special agent.** In some circumstances and complicated games, the use of agencies and intermediaries can complement the sports marketer and his team's regular work very effectively. Although, in the world of football, the presence of intermediaries tends to generate mistrust, the fact is that the involvement of these 'special agents' can help you to get more money, especially in situations such as:
  ▸ The need to bring in revenue in a very short space of time.
  ▸ Sales for specific one-off projects or projects that need to be commercially exploited on a sporadic or very infrequent basis (for example, the sale of television rights).
  ▸ Activities or products with a low sales potential that does not justify having one's own sales force.
  ▸ Negotiations for big projects that require absolute confidentiality or that involve having conversations with the competitors of the sports property's sponsors or strategic partners.
  ▸ Potential clients located in distant places.

The involvement of specialist agencies and intermediaries has the great advantage of not incurring any fixed costs for the sports property, because commonly their fee is 100 per cent performance-linked in the form of sales commissions. But you will need to closely analyse the credentials of the agencies and intermediaries that offer to bring you new clients, especially if they require sales exclusivity (for specific geographical areas or limited periods of time), which agents generally do request.

THE FIRST ELEVEN AND THE TECHNICAL STAFF

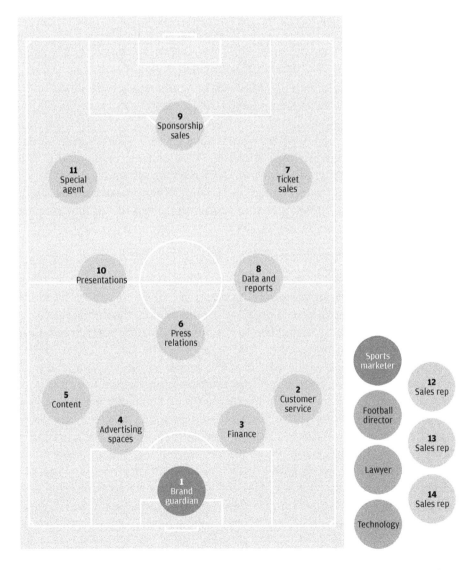

On the bench, alongside the substitute sales staff, you should surround yourself with the very best technical staff. First, the **football director**, with whom you really need to be on the same wavelength so that you can get continued engagement from players in commercial activities. Another vital element is the work of the **lawyer,** who will be in charge of drawing up contracts and ensuring that they are followed from a legal point of view. Neither must we forget the **technology manager,** who will ensure that the relevant servers and websites are all working, along with the online ticket sales software and the switchboard that will take members' calls.

Eleven sales techniques that work

In June 2011, Bayer Leverkusen of the German Bundesliga placed a desperate ad in the international edition of the *Financial Times*, in its search for a shirt sponsor for the 2011/12 season. Under the title 'Come and play the Champions League with us! This is your opportunity to become our main sponsor', the advert invited companies from all over the world to bid for this sponsorship package.

I don't know if Sunpower, the brand that Bayer 04 Leverkusen ended up displaying on its shirts during the 2011/12 season, responded to this innovative initiative, but I do think that there are more effective and definitely more economic sales and negotiation techniques out there. Let's now look at some of the sales techniques that I have been able to put into practice during my career as a sports marketer.

❶ Get the money

When I was a teenager, now and again I would help out at my family's jewellery shop in Lleida in Spain and my parents would say, 'The first thing you need to ask the customer on the other side of the counter is what their budget is; from that moment on, your goal must be to ensure that the customer doesn't leave the shop *without having spent at least the sum he told you.*'

This very basic technique can also be applied in sports marketing. So whenever a company approaches you expressing an interest in one of your products, you should try your damnedest to not let him leave 'without buying anything'. Let's suppose for a moment that a potential client has asked about a sponsorship package that is outside their budget. After asking a few questions to get a better understanding of his needs, you should try to offer some alternatives that will allow you to get that money anyway. For example, as long as it doesn't close the door to future sponsors from the same industry that are willing to buy the whole package, you could suggest a sponsorship package with less content, single advertising spaces or even a VIP box at the stadium.

❷ Neighbouring sponsors

One of the factors that are instrumental when a sponsor selects a sports property is the profile of the other brands that are already sponsoring it. It is a proven fact that the big companies want neighbours of the same level or higher, but never lower. This was the main argument we decided to use to convince Audi to form part of FC Barcelona's sponsorship programme. We were more flexible in the negotiations on the monetary sums because we felt that the prestige of the brand would be an advertisement for attracting other brands into our sponsorship programme.

So I suggest that you identify companies that, as well as adding sheen to your sponsorship programme, can act as a 'hook' to reel in more sponsors, even if this means having to accept a lower fee.

❸ Imitating Apple

It is really fascinating to see how, launch after launch, Apple manages to create a sense that there are very few units of its new product available, so the consumers who want it must hurry and stand in long queues to get it. It is not necessary that the entire product range has been sold out in order to create a sense of scarcity and increase the consumers' urge to lay their hands on it. For example, news that stocks of the 16GB iPad2 (the most affordable model in the range) had run out will create the same effect without losing sales because the demand can be redirected towards other models in the range (at a higher price, of course).

In some situations, you will have the chance to replicate the 'Apple effect' during the process of commercially exploiting your sports property's products: for example, in ticket and membership sales, by selling out certain areas of the stadium or matches that will be played later in the season; when selling VIP boxes and hospitality packages, by notifying clients that some of the best boxes are already taken; and even when selling sponsorship programmes, by not letting new brands in to some of the categories once you have reached the maximum number you initially set yourself. Your objective as a sports marketer will always be to generate news that create a sense of scarcity and to make as much noise as possible in the media so that this news reaches your potential customers.

❹ Side with the enemy

'If you can't beat 'em, join 'em.' The old adage can sometimes inspire you to identify ways of getting money from companies that want to associate themselves with a particular sports property but without intending to buy any of its commercial products. Brands that repeatedly run adverts in the section dedicated to a sports property in the media; brands that create ambush marketing campaigns; or even the brands that illegally use the registered trademarks of a sports property in their advertising: all of these are ideal candidates (as long as they are not competitors of your main sponsor) to whom you can present the benefits of forming part of the sponsorship programme or of buying advertising from the sports property in a totally legitimate manner.

❺ Make the most of the sporting momentum

However powerful and successful a football team may be, it is usually the case that victories are cyclical in nature and that at some point they make way for failure (or the success of our eternal rivals). At FC Barcelona, for example, we took advantage of the international pulling power of the team after it had won two consecutive Ligas (2004/05 and 2005/06) and a Champions League (2006) to intensify our commercial efforts and sign as many contracts as possible. So, in that period of time, we signed the best contracts of my career at the club, including those of Nike, Audi and Mediapro (TV rights). Some contracts were renewed without being close to termination. Because of this, the club continued to see its revenue grow even when it went through a bad patch, winning no titles in two consecutive seasons (2006/07 and 2007/08).

So if you can take advantage of the winning streaks to push through renewals of long-term contracts (even if they are not yet due to end) and bring in new clients, you will be instrumental in making your sports property's revenue more immune to poor sports results which, whether you like it or not, will inevitably come, sooner or later.

EVOLUTION OF FC BARCELONA'S REVENUE IN COMPARISON TO TITLES WON

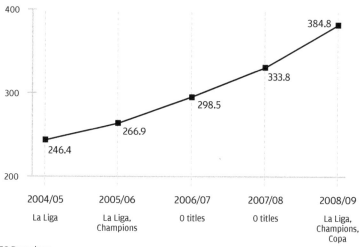

Source: FC Barcelona
Figures in millions of euros
Not including sales of players

❻ To-ing and fro-ing

Often, after long negotiation processes, we realise that we can go no further. The client has put forward a sum and we know for a fact that he won't agree to anything higher. But this doesn't mean you should give up, because in this final stage of to-ing and fro-ing, you can improve the profitability of an agreement considerably. For example, in sponsorship negotiations in which you have not managed to reach the yearly sum that you had set yourself as a target, you can (and should) try things such as securing longer-term contracts, including fewer benefits or giving exclusivity to fewer countries or industries. In this way, you can get more money from the same client (with a longer-term contract) or free up content that you can then offer to other potential clients.

❼ Bootlicking

Any lawful tools that the sports marketer can come up with are valid, when it comes to buttering up the client. Don't forget that a satisfied customer will always speak well of you out there in the marketplace (and at the end of the day, this will help you to attract new clients) and will be more willing to renew the contract in terms that are more favourable to us. The age-old technique of buttering up consists of going out of one's way to give the best possible service to the customer. One can give them (and their guests) VIP treatment during their stadium experience; now and again offer additional content without asking for payment; provide samples of their media appearances; send them a signed shirt for their child's birthday; take their suggestions for how to improve the sponsorship programme into account; or share relevant reports that you have gained access to. With all this, you will be instrumental in ensuring that the way a partnership with your sports property is evaluated is not based solely and exclusively on a cold analysis of the return on investment figures.

❽ The swap shop

The exchange of products and services is a model that is fully operational in the sport business, especially in environments that are seeing a general economic downturn. There's no doubt that it's much easier to attract a client when you can offer them the possibility of 'paying' for a sports property's products in kind instead of in cash. At FC Barcelona, we managed to achieve significant cost-cutting (with a net impact on the profit and loss accounts that was identical to that made by sales) through sponsorship agreements signed solely on a quid pro quo basis. Companies such as Endesa, Gas Natural or NH Hotels got some of the benefits of sponsorship in exchange for giving us energy services and hotel rooms for team trips.

So don't miss that opportunity to conduct a detailed analysis of your sports property's costs. Items such as printers and ink cartridges, courier services, mobile phones, car hire or flight tickets will help you to draw up an alternative list of sponsorship candidates or potential buyers of hospitality packages, from which you can get some pretty impressive sales figures.

❾ Juggle more than one bid

Being in a position to threaten a potential client with accepting another company's bid for the same product is both an effective sales technique and a moment of pleasure for the sports marketer. It is therefore very important that during the negotiation and sales process you try with every means possible to open up several lines of negotiation and if you do, to try to keep them all active until the last minute, even in the last stages of negotiation with the client that's best positioned to get the product. The candidate should know that you have other offers and that you're also prepared to accept them. So until you have formally signed an agreement, do not rush to tell other bidders that you have decided to accept another proposal. Obviously, this technique is only meaningful if you do really have other offers. I don't recommend that you bluff, pretending to have bids that actually don't exist. In the end, you will be found out and this will damage your own and your sports property's reputation in the market.

❿ Higher price

There's no worse feeling when selling than finding out that we have offered a lower price than what the customer was willing to pay. This situation, which can arise when selling sports property products that don't have an 'official' price (such as sponsorship packages, for example), can be avoided by conducting a proper analysis of the potential customer beforehand and by asking the right questions during the negotiation process. You should therefore seek out information on other sponsorship investments that the client has made and on his budget and be very astute at every meeting, to try to pick up clues that will help you to figure out the price he has in his head. Remember that once you've told him a price, you can't do anything to raise it. So, if in doubt, always try to give a price that's at the upper end of your expectations.

⓫ The big slogan

After a dreadful start to the Serie A 2011/12 season, Inter Milan managed to make its way back up to the top positions of the table, thanks to a phenomenal purple patch of consecutive wins. This spectacular comeback became the perfect excuse for the club's sports marketers to launch a new season ticket holders campaign for the second round of the competition, which they called 'the big comeback', with full-page adverts in the main Italian newspapers. In March 2007, Real Madrid was fourth in La Liga table, five points behind joint leaders FC Barcelona and Sevilla. With the media on-side, it decided to drive a campaign under the slogan 'Together, we can', with which it aimed to mobilise the entire club fan base to help it get back up and win the title. Rewarded with great sporting results (Real Madrid did eventually lift the trophy), the club's sports marketers enjoyed an exceptional window of opportunity in which to sell sponsorship, tickets and hospitality packages, among other things.

Identifying milestones or special circumstances that are able to mobilise the public may well be the best sales technique there is. Even without having to develop campaigns relating to victories on the pitch, you will be able to get great results on every front, capitalising on situations such as the countdown to the day you move to a new stadium, the chance to hit a magic number or overtaking your eternal rivals in membership numbers.

Remember that to make the most of this technique, you need to bear three important factors in mind: (1) that the slogan chosen for the campaign has to be based on an achievable goal; (2) that the media has to be falling over itself to publicise it; and (3) that it has to be used in special circumstances that are not often repeated.

Eleven skills for winning the Ballon d'Or

With a genuine dream team, a bench with exceptional sales staff, a technical team willing to give it their all, the very best sales techniques available to you and a sports property with a commercial product, you have everything you need to win the sports marketer's Ballon d'Or. All you need to add to that mix is the extra ingredient that only you can provide, with your attitude and your style.

The Ballon d'Or sports marketer should be …

❶ **Proactive.** Tries to set up as many meetings and create as many sales opportunities as possible.

❷ **Backed up by documents.** Puts forward the sales pitch using objective data.

❸ **Well informed.** Up to date with current regulations and what's happening in the market, reading the press regularly and subscribing to a range of publications.

❹ **Rational.** Only invests time into matters that they are able to influence.

❺ **Creative.** Brings new ideas and new ways of doing things.

❻ **Observant.** Identifies ideas that are being used by other sports properties and applies them to his or her own properties.

❼ **Generous.** Offers strategic clients more benefits that those stipulated in the contracts, working with them to help them translate their investment into business.

⑧ **Well connected.** Has a large book of contacts, and takes time to maintain and expand it with extensive travelling and social activities.

⑨ **Accessible.** Success does not go to their head, and they try to make themselves available even to the smallest clients.

⑩ **Rigorous.** Documents decisions, formalises agreements as contracts, oversees compliance and reports infringements.

⑪ **A footie fan.** Follows football and is a regular consumer of football content in the media.

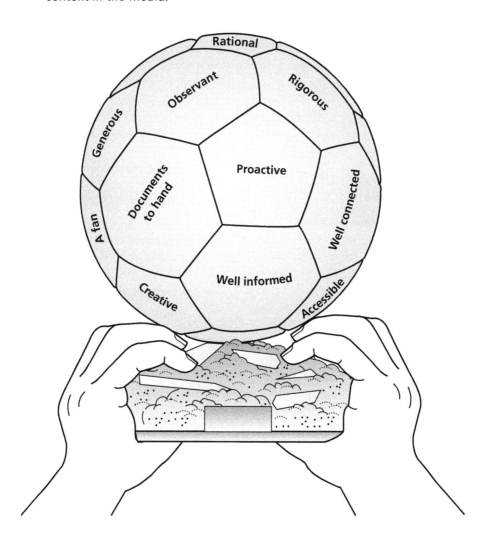

The eleven files in the new minister's briefcase

In Spain, when the Prime Minister appoints a new minister, an act of protocol is organised in which the outgoing minister hands over his briefcase to the incoming minister. This act is intended to symbolise the transfer of authority between the two, and the idea is that the briefcase holds the basic documentation that the new minister will need to start his new job, alongside the questions that he will obviously be able to ask his predecessor in meetings.

My departure from FC Barcelona was not too traumatic because the club decided to put Daniel Schloesser in my position, and he was already a member of my team and the commercial director. So we didn't need too many information transfer meetings because Daniel and I had been working together for several years. Nevertheless, we decided to capture the moment I transferred authority to him by taking an amusing picture of me handing him the factbook (the equivalent of the briefcase) where I had filed the most important data relating to all the club's projects.

JUNE 2007: HANDING OVER THE FACTBOOK TO THE NEW CHIEF
MARKETING OFFICER AT FC BARCELONA

The day you've been waiting for has arrived and you are getting ready to start your new job as a sports marketer. Behind you lies a long pre-season of preparation and a long selection process, in which you have managed to beat all your rivals to the position. You are about to enter your new office at the sports property and you have the chance to meet with your predecessor. You ask them for the 'minister's briefcase' and, as a sports marketer that has completed their training with flying colours, you ask if it contains the following files:

❶ Positioning statement.
❷ List of all the registered trademarks and distinguishing symbols.
❸ Profit and loss accounts and business plan.
❹ A file of press cuttings.
❺ The supporter numbers kit.
❻ Historical statistics on match attendance.
❼ Action plan for ticket sales.
❽ Map of the stadium with the location and prices of different ticket and season ticket categories.
❾ Copy of all the contacts and a summary of their most important contents.
❿ Sponsorship sales dossier.
⓫ List and contact details of all the main contacts.

Whether all the files that you would ideally like to find are there or not (generally, not), your first task is to carefully study all the information available on your sports property, whether it has been provided to you beforehand or whether you have to ask for it yourself. Bear in mind that the faster you familiarise yourself with your sports property's past, the faster you can start out on a new route that will take you to where that money is.

So, pick up your roadmap and get ready to start the official season. You're in shape and well prepared. No excuses. *Show me the money*, sports marketer! The sooner, the better.

Bibliography

SHANK, Matthew D. *Sports Marketing: A Strategic Perspective*. Pearson Prentice Hall.

MASTERALEXIS, Lisa P., BARR, Carol A., HUMS, Mary A. *Principles and Practice of Sport Management*. Jones and Bartlett.

SPOELSTRA, Jon. *How to Sell the Last Seat in the House*. www.jonspoelstra.com.

GRAHAM, Stedman, NEIROTTI, Lisa, GOLDBLATT, Joe. *The Ultimate Guide to Sports Marketing*. McGraw-Hill.

Global Sports Media Consumption Report 2011. Perform, TV Sports Markets & KantarSport.

Deloitte Football Money League www.deloitte.com

Football Transfer Review www.primetimesport.com

SportBusiness www.sportbusiness.com

SportsPro www.sportspromedia.com

Acknowledgements

To my first team at FC Barcelona: Cristina Vázquez, Julián Fernández, Patricia Plasencia, Dolors Romero, Omar Berrada, James Sene, Eva González, Jordi Vilanova and Xavier Comerma.

To other colleagues at FC Barcelona: Daniel Schloesser, Antonio Martín, Laura González, Joshua Thomson, Pablo Negre, Javier Muñoa, Cristina Mora, Josep Maria Meseguer, Francesc Lladós, Vanessa Basora, José Rey, Marisa Casillas, Mireia Cierco, Montse Quílez, Olga Fernández, Txiki Begiristain, Raúl Sanllehí, Ramón Pujol, Josep Vergés, Oriol Ràfols, Josep Llorca, Toni Ruiz, Txemi Terés, Carlos Naval, Sofía Moya and Ingo Sonego.

To Ferran Soriano and Marc Ingla, who, as directors, played a decisive role in developing and professionalising the marketing function at FC Barcelona.

To everyone who was on the board of directors at FC Barcelona between 2002 and 2007.

To Javier Pérez Farguell, my first boss at FC Barcelona, who gave me the wonderful opportunity of working for my beloved Barça and taking my first steps in sports marketing.

To Jon Banks, Albert Baronet, Marcos Garzo, Carlos Homedes, Guillermo Fadda, Jaume Alemany, Carles Casanovas, Javier Mas and David Chías, as representatives of companies that were so committed in their sponsorship of FC Barcelona.

To my colleagues at Prime Time Sport: Bruno Batlle, Aleix Piqué and Valeria López.

To Libros de Cabecera, for their commitment to this project from the outset.

To Roger Domingo, who was my student on the Sports Marketing Insights module I taught for the MBA at ESADE, and who was the first person to suggest that I write a book on the subject.

To ESADE, where I was fortunate enough to study and in the library of which most of this book was written.

To The Killers and their song 'Human', a source of inspiration throughout the writing of this book.

Index

www.ingramcontent.com/pod-product-compliance
Ingram Content Group UK Ltd.
Pitfield, Milton Keynes, MK11 3LW, UK
UKHW040640280225
455688UK00002B/39